THE ROYAL COURT
THEATRE PRESENTS

G000270369

Roald Dahl's

THE
TWITS

Mischievously adapted by
Enda Walsh

Roald Dahl's

THE TWITS

Mischievously adapted by ENDA WALSH

CAST (in alphabetical order)

Yorkshire Terrier Man **Sam Cox**
Monkey Mum **Cait Davis**
Mrs Twit **Monica Dolan**
Monkey Daughter **Aimée-Ffion Edwards**
Tatooed Fortune Teller Lady **Christine Entwisle**
Monkey Son **Oliver Llewellyn-Jenkins**
Monkey Father **Glyn Pritchard**
Handsome Waltzer Boy **Dwane Walcott**
Mr Twit **Jason Watkins**

Director **John Tiffany**
Associate Director/Movement **Steven Hoggett**
Composer & Musical Supervisor **Martin Lowe**
Designer **Chloe Lamford**
Lighting Designer **Philip Gladwell**
Sound Designer **Gregory Clarke**
Music Production **Phij Adams**
Associate Director **Katy Rudd**
Associate Movement Director **Vicki Manderson**
Associate Designer **Fly Davis**
Casting Director **Amy Ball**
Production Manager **Niall Black**
Costume Supervisor **Lucy Walshaw**
Company Manager **Heidi Lennard**
Stage Manager **Rebecca Maltby**
Deputy Stage Manager **Sarah Hellicar**
Assistant Stage Manager **Greg Sharman**
Stage Management Work Placement **Libbie Khabaza**
Set Constructed by **Miraculous Engineering**
Set Painted by **Lisa Dickson, Sarah Hrida, Kerry Jarrett**

Special thanks to **Charmian Hoare & Stephen Harper**

The Royal Court & Stage Management wish to thank the following for their help with this production:
Almeida, Arjobex Polyart, Charlie Ash, James Boston, Charles Dickens Primary School
Southwark, Donmar Warehouse, GlassEyes.com, Globe Theatre, Jess Jones, Elinor Keber, Eilidh
Macleod, Opera Holland Park, Annie Price, Queen's Theatre Hornchurch, Regent's Park Open
Air Theatre, The Roald Dahl Museum & Story Centre, in particular Tricia Croot & Rachel White,
Suzanna Rosenthal, RSC, St Benedict's Jr School Ealing, Young Vic.

THE TWITS
THE COMPANY

Roald Dahl (Writer)

Roald Dahl was born in Cardiff in 1916 and at the age of 23 joined the RAF. He began writing after a plane crash in which he suffered serious injuries.

Sitting in a hut at the bottom of his garden – surrounded by odd bits and pieces such as a suitcase full of logs (which he used as a footrest), his own hipbone (which he'd had replaced) and a heavy ball of metal foil (made from years' worth of chocolate wrappers) – Roald Dahl wrote classics such as CHARLIE AND THE CHOCOLATE FACTORY, THE BFG, MATILDA and lots more!

Roald Dahl Day is celebrated on 13 September every year, on what would have been his birthday. His many books remain as popular as ever. To discover more visit www.roalddahl.com.

Enda Walsh (Mischievous Adapter)

As Writer, theatre includes: **Room 303** (Galway International Arts Festival); Ballyturk, Misterman (Landmark/Galway International Arts Festival); Once (West End/Broadway/Worldwide); My Friend Duplicity, Bedbound (Traverse); Penelope, The Walworth Farce (Druid); Chatroom (National); The New Electric Ballroom (Kammerspiele, Munich); The Small Things (Paines Plough/Menier Chocolate Factory); Disco Pigs (Corcadorca/Trishel Arts).

As Writer, film includes: **Hunger, Disco Pigs.**

As Writer, radio includes: **Four Big Days in the Life of Dessie Banks. The Monotonous Life of Little Miss P.**

Awards include: **Tony Award, Outer Critic Circle Award, Lortel (Once); Fringe First (Disco Pigs, Bedbound, The Walworth Farce, The New Electric Ballroom, Penelope); Irish Times Theatre Award for Best Production (Ballyturk); Honorary Doctorate Degree from Galway University.**

Phij Adams (Music Production)

As Programmer, theatre includes: **The Producers, Shrek (UK tour); Women on the Verge of a Nervous Breakdown, Made in Dagenham, Memphis, Charlie & the Chocolate Factory, A Chorus Line, Sweeney Todd, Imagine This, Closer to Heaven (West End); Elf The Musical (Bord Gáis Energy, Dublin); Anything Goes, Me & My Girl (Sheffield); Matilda (RSC/West End/Broadway); Loserville (West End/West Yorkshire Playhouse/Top Hat/UK tour); Ragtime (Regent's Park Open Air); Singin' In The Rain (West End/UK tour/Japan); Ghost (West End/UK tour/Broadway/Korea); The Secret Garden (Edinburgh International Festival/Toronto Festival); Sweet Charity (Menier Chocolate Factory/West End); The Lord of the Rings (West End/Toronto); Bombay Dreams (West End/Broadway); Guys & Dolls (West End/UK tour/Australia tour); Edward Scissorhands, The Car Man, Dorian Gray (Matthew Bourne); Der Scuh des Manitu (Theater de Westens, Berlin).**

Gregory Clarke (Sound Designer)

For the Royal Court: **The Ritual Slaughter of Gorge Mastromas.**

Other theatre includes: **Medea, The Doctor's Dilemma, Misterman, Twelfth Night, No Man's Land, Tristan & Yseult, The Emperor Jones, Earthquakes in London (National); My Night With Reg, Versailles, The Night Alive, A Voyage Around My Father, The Philanthropist (Donmar); The Merchant Of Venice, Cloud Nine (Almeida); All's Well That Ends Well, The Heart of Robin Hood, Great Expectations, Coriolanus, The Merry Wives of Windsor, Tantalus, Cymbeline, A Midsummer Night's Dream (RSC); Clarence Darrow, A Flea In Her Ear, National Anthems, Six Degrees of Separation (Old Vic); Journey's End, Equus (West End/Broadway); Annie Get Your Gun (UK tour); The Boy In The Striped Pajamas (Chichester Festival/Children's Touring Partnership); The Birthday Party (Royal Exchange, Manchester); The Seagull (Headlong); Assassins, Two Into One, The Lyons, The Color Purple, Travels With My Aunt, Proof (Menier Chocolate Factory); Donkeys' Years (Rose, Kingston); Arcadia (ETT); Tonight At 8.30 (Nuffield/ETT); Ciphers (Out Of Joint); Another Place, Solid Air (Theatre Royal, Plymouth); A Steady Rain (Theatre Royal, Bath);**

The Little Mermaid (Bristol Old Vic); Brigit, Bailegangaire (Druid); The Night Alive, The Philanthropist, Pygmalion (Broadway); My Night With Reg, Goodnight Mr Tom, The Vortex, A Voyage Around My Father, And Then There Were None, Some Girls, Waiting for Godot, What The Butler Saw (West End).

Awards include: **Drama Desk Award for Outstanding Sound Design (Journey's End); Tony Award for best sound design of a play (Equus).**

Sam Cox (Yorkshire Terrier Man)

Theatre includes: **Man, My Dad's a Birdman (Young Vic); Henry V, The Tempest, Gabriel, Julius Caesar, Doctor Scroggy's War, 'Tis Pity She's a Whore, All's Well That Ends Well, Anne Boleyn, Henry VIII (Globe); The Trojan Woman (Gate); Lovesong (Frantic Assembly); The Deep Blue Sea (West Yorkshire); Inherit the Wind (Old Vic); Arcadia (West End); Edward Gant's Amazing Feats of Loneliness (Headlong/UK tour/Soho/Drum, Plymouth); Oedipus, The UN Inspector (National); So Close to Home (Arcola); On Religion (British Council); God in Ruins, Macbeth, King John, Henry V, Romeo & Juliet, Richard II, Toilus & Cressida, (RSC); Shrieks of Laughter (Soho); Tintin (Barbican); Festen (Almeida/West End).**

Television includes: **Borgia, Doctors, New Tricks, The Commander, The Inspector Lynley Mysteries, Doctor Who, The Last Will & Testament of Billy Two Sheds, Holby City, The Murder Of Stephen Lawrence, The Wings Of Angels, London Bridge, Peak Practice, Crime Traveller, Madson, Back Up, Prime Suspect, Kavanagh QC, The Chief, Dandelion Dead, The Bill, Foreign Affairs, The Orchid House, Die Kinder, Bergerac, Blind Justice, Dead Head, McKenzie, The Chinese Detective.**

Film includes: **King of Soho, Wall, Anna Karenina, Agora, Hippie Hippie Shake, Call at Coracon.**

Radio includes: **Festen.**

Cait Davis (Monkey Mum)

Theatre includes: **Electra (Old Vic); The Jungle Book (West Yorkshire Playhouse); pool (no water), Dirty Wonderland, Sellout, Zero, Flesh, Klub (Frantic Assembly);**

The Wolves in the Wall (National Theatre of Scotland/Lyric, Hammersmith/tour); The Little Fir Tree (Crucible); Measure for Measure (National); Top Girl (Citizens, Glasgow); Those Eyes, That Mouth, Fermentation (Grid Iron); The Chimp That Spoke, Mosquito Coast (Young Vic/tour); How to Behave (Station Opera House/Hampstead); Running Girl, Red (Boilerhouse); 1984 (Northern Stage Ensemble); Phantom Limb (Gargantua); Into Our Dreams (Almeida); Scratch (20:21); The Carrier Frequency (Stan's Café); Walking to Whiteway (Everyman, Cheltenham).

Television includes: **Doctors, Respectable Trade.**

Fly Davis (Associate Designer)

As Designer, for the Royal Court: **Pigeons, Collaboration, Primetime.**

As Associate Designer, for the Royal Court: **Open Court Season, No Quarter, Disconnect.**

As Designer, theatre includes: **Scuttlers, Hunger for Trade (Royal Exchange, Manchester); James & The Giant Peach (WYP); I'd Rather Goya Robbed Me of My Sleep Than Some Other Arsehole (Gate); Superior Donuts (Southwark Playhouse); The Dissidents (Tricycle); Streetcar Parallel, Turn a Little Further (Young Vic); Khadija is 18, Almost Near, The Man (Finborough); What the Animals Say (Greyscale); The Great British Country Fête (Bush/UK tour); England Street (Oxford Playhouse); Life Support (Theatre Royal York); Woyzeck (Omnibus).**

Music Videos include: **Love is Easy (McFly).**

Monica Dolan (Mrs Twit)

For the Royal Court: **Birth of a Nation, Sliding with Suzanne (& Out of Joint), The Glory of Living**

Other theatre includes: **The Same Deep Water as Me (Donmar); Chalet Lines (Bush); King Lear, The Seagull, The Taming of the Shrew, A Midsummer Night's Dream (RSC); Jane Eyre (Shared Experience tour/West End); Macbeth (Out of Joint); Mary Stuart (Nuffield, Southampton); She Stoops to Conquer, A Laughing Matter (National/Out of Joint); The Walls (National); Hayfever (Triumph Proscenium); The Glass Menagerie (Royal Lyceum, Edinburgh).**

Television includes: **W1A, The Casual Vacancy, Wolf Hall, The Escape Artist, Complicit, Call the Midwife, Coming Up, Appropriate Adult, U Be Dead, Excluded, Inspector Banks, Occupation, Midsomer Murders, The History of Mr Polly, Poirot, The Commander, Wallis & Edward, Tipping the Velvet, Judge John Deed, The Gift.**

Film includes: **Eye in the Sky, Pride, The Falling, Alpha Papa, Sightseers, The Arbor, Never Let Me Go, Within the Whirlwind, King Lear, Topsy Turvy, A Midsummer Night's Dream.**

Awards include: **BAFTA for Best Supporting Actress (Appropriate Adult).**

Aimée-Ffion Edwards (Monkey Daughter)

For the Royal Court: **Jerusalem (& Music Box, New York/West End).**

Other theatre includes: **Trelawny of the Wells, The Recruiting Officer (Donmar); Fireface (Young Vic); Shitmix (Trafalgar); Under Milk Wood, Matchmaker (Newport Playgoers); An Informer's Duty, Bottecelli's Bonfire (National Youth Theatre of Wales); Les Misérables (URDD Youth); Planted Plant (S4C/Welsh tour); The Glass Menagerie (Dolman Solo).**

Television includes: **Bugsplat, Detectorists, Wolf Hall, Under Milk Wood, Peaky Blinders, Flack, A Poet in New York, Inside Number 9, Walking & Talking, Luther, Little Crackers – Better than Christmas, Being Human, Law & Order, Casualty 1909, Casualty, Skins, Y Pris, Wawffactor, The Rough Guide, Mad, Bad & Dangerous.**

Film includes: **Steak Knife, Queen & Country, One Day, Epithet.**

Radio includes: **Une Vie, Cordite for Breakfast, Burning Up, Plantagenet.**

Christine Entwisle (Tattooed Fortune Teller Lady)

For the Royal Court: **Hope, Primetime, Narrative, The Wonderful World of Dissocia (& Tron/Drum, Plymouth/Edinburgh International Festival/tour), Gamblers.**

Other theatre includes: **Billy the Girl (Clean Break/Soho); Titus (Theory of Everything); As You Like It, The Comedy of Errors, Romeo & Juliet, Silence, The Drunks, Morte D'Athur (RSC);**

Six Characters in Search of an Author (West End/Headlong/Chichester Festival); Half Life (National Theatre of Scotland); C'est Vauxhall! (Duckie/Barbican); Genetics for Blondes (Soho); The Wedding (Southwark Playhouse/National tour); Vassa (Almeida/The Albery); A Family Affair (Clwyd); Wonderhorse (Edinburgh International Festival/ICA/BAC); Edward Gant's Amazing Feats of Loneliness (UK tour/Soho/Drum, Plymouth); I Am Dandy (Purcell Rooms/BAC); Ubu Kunst, Missing Jesus (Young Vic); Paper Walls (Scarlet/Assembly Rooms/Purcell Rooms); Fine (Young Vic/Edinburgh International Festival); People Shows 100–103 (International tour).

Television includes: **Attachments, Holby City, Where the Heart Is, Dalziel & Pascoe.**

Film includes: **Mothers & Daughters, At Dawning, Storm Damage, Deeper Still.**

Radio includes: **Heredity, Doyouwishtocontinue.**

Awards include: **BBC Writers Award (Doyouwishtocontinue); Critics Award for Theatre in Scotland for Best Actress, Tron Best Actress Award (The Wonderful World of Dissocia).**

Philip Gladwell (Lighting Designer)

For the Royal Court: **Liberian Girl, God Bless the Child, The Ritual Slaughter of Gorge Mastromas, No Quarter, Oxford Street, Kebab.**

Other theatre includes: **The James Plays (& National Theatre of Scotland), The World of Extreme Happiness, Love the Sinner (National); The Sound of Music, Hairspray, Chicago, Obama the Mamba, Gypsy (Leicester Curve); The Infidel (Theatre Royal Stratford East); Mr Burns, Before the Party (Almeida); Happy Days, The King & I, Radio Times (UK tour); Ciara, I'm With the Band, The Arthur Conan Doyle Appreciation Society (Traverse); LIMBO (London Wonderground & International tour); Miss Julie (Barbican/Schaubühne, Berlin); A Midsummer Night's Dream (Barbican/Bristol Old Vic/Spoleto Festival, USA); Enjoy (West Yorkshire Playhouse); Pastoral (Soho); The Opinion Makers (Mercury, Colchester/Derby); Every Last Trick, One For the Road, The Duchess of Malfi, Blood Wedding (Royal & Derngate); If Only (Chichester Festival); Further Than the Furthest Thing (Dundee Rep);**

Amazonia, Ghosts, The Member of the Wedding, Festa! (Young Vic); Cinderella, Aladdin, Mogadishu, Punk Rock (Lyric Hammersmith); Too Clever By Half, You Can't Take It With You, Nineteen Eighty-Four, Macbeth (Royal Exchange, Manchester); The Fahrenheit Twins, Low Pay? Don't Pay! (Told by an Idiot).

Steven Hoggett (Associate Director/Movement)

For the Royal Court: **Let the Right One In (& National Theatre of Scotland/West End/St. Ann's, New York).**

As Choreographer, theatre includes: **The Last Ship, The Curious Incident Of The Dog In The Night-Time (& West End), Rocky: The Musical, The Glass Menagerie, Once (& West End), Green Day's American Idiot, Peter & The Starcatcher (Broadway); The Light Princess, Dido Queen of Carthage, The Hothouse, Market Boy (National); The Full Monty (Sheffield Lyceum/UK tour); 365, The Bacchae (& associate director), The Wolves in the Wall (& Improbable), Black Watch (& associate director) (National Theatre of Scotland); Mercury Fur, The Straits (Paines Plough).**

As Director, theatre includes: **War Correspondents (Helen Chadwick); What's It All About (New York Theatre Workshop); Lovesong, Beautiful Burnout (& National Theatre of Scotland), Othello, Frankenstein, Stockholm, pool (no water), Dirty Wonderland, Rabbit, Peepshow, Heavenly, Tiny Dynamite (& Paines Plough), Underworld, Vs. (& Karim Tonsey), Sell Out, Zero, Flesh, Klub, Look Back in Anger (Frantic Assembly); Air (MAC); Service Charge (Lyric, Hammersmith).**

As Director, opera includes: **Dalston Songs (ROH).**

As choreographer, opera includes: **Rigoletto (Met); Dr Dee (ENO/Manchester International Festival).**

As Choreographer, film includes: **How To Train Your Dragon 2.**

Awards include: **Laurence Olivier Award for Best Theatre Choreographer (Black Watch); Lortel, Obie and Calloway Awards for Best Choreography (Once).**

Steven was founder and co-artistic director of Frantic Assembly. He has provided choreography for Prada, Radio 1 and Orange as well as music promos for Goldfrapp, Calvin Harris, Bat for Lashes and Franz Ferdinand. With Scott Graham, he co-wrote The Frantic Assembly Book of Devising Theatre (Routledge).

Chloe Lamford (Designer)

For the Royal Court: **How to Hold Your Breath, God Bless the Child, 2071, Teh Internet is Serious Business, Open Court, Circle Mirror Transformation.**

Other theatre includes: **Salt Root & Roe (Donmar/Trafalgar Studios); Praxis Makes Perfect (National Theatre Wales); Lungs (Schaubühne, Berlin); 1984 (Headlong/Almeida/West End/ tour); Rules for Living, The World of Extreme Happiness (National); Boys (Headlong); Cannibals, The Gate Keeper (Royal Exchange, Manchester); The Events (Actors Touring Company/ Young Vic/tour); The History Boys (Crucible, Sheffield); Disco Pigs, Sus, Blackta (Young Vic); My Shrinking Life, An Appointment With the Wicker Man, Knives in Hens (National Theatre of Scotland); The Radicalisation of Bradley Manning (National Theatre Wales/Edinburgh International Festival); Ghost Story (Sky Arts Live Drama); Britannicus (Wilton's Music Hall); My Romantic History (Crucible, Sheffield/Bush); Joseph K, The Kreutzer Sonata (Gate); Songs From A Hotel Bedroom (ROH/tour); it felt empty when the heart went at first but it is alright now, This Wide Night (Clean Break); The Mother Ship, How to Tell the Monsters from the Misfits (Birmingham Rep); Small Miracle (Tricycle/Mercury, Colchester).**

Awards Include: **Theatrical Management Association Award for Best Theatre Design (Small Miracle); Arts Foundation Fellowship Award for Design for Performance: Set & Costume.**

Oliver Llewellyn-Jenkins (Monkey Son)

Theatre includes: **World Cup Final 1966 (Bristol Old Vic); Wanted! Robin Hood (Library); The History Boys (Mercury, Colchester); Batman Live (World tour); The Resistible Rise of Arturo Ui (West Glamorgan Youth); The Dreaming (National Youth).**

Television includes: **Doctors, Poets of the Somme, Stella, The Story of Tracy Beaker, Care.**

Film includes: **Carrie's War, The Tulse Luper Suitcase Trilogy.**

Martin Lowe (Composer & Musical Supervisor)

For the Royal Court: **Hope.**

Other theatre includes: **Once (Broadway/ West End/Melbourne); Jedermann (Salzburg Festival); The Light Princess, War Horse, Caroline or Change, Jerry Springer The Opera, A Funny Thing Happened on the way to the Forum, Nation (National); The Lily's Revenge, (American Repertory); Appointment with the Wicker Man, The Wolves in the Walls (National Theatre of Scotland) Mamma Mia! (West End/Shanghai, Tokyo/Seoul/International tour/ Stockholm), The Full Monty, Once on this Island, Cats, Les Misérables (West End).**

Composition includes: **The Misanthrope, The Secret Rapture, Hysteria(Chichester Festival); The Blue Room (Minerva/West End); Lettice & Lovage (UK Tour); Into Exile, Dear Exile (BBC).**

Orchestration includes: **Once, The Light Princess, Once in a Lifetime (National) Loserville (West End).**

Recordings include: **Once, Mamma Mia! The Movie, Jedermann, Jerry Springer The Opera, Mamma Mia!**

Film includes: **Mamma Mia! The Movie, Greetings From Tim Buckley.**

Awards include: **Tony, Olivier, Grammy, Drama Desk, Obie Award (Once); Golden Reel Award (Mamma Mia! The Movie).**

Vicki Manderson (Associate Movement Director)

For the Royal Court: **Let the Right One In (& National Theatre of Scotland/West End/St Ann's, New York).**

As Movement Director, theatre includes: **Details (Grid Iron); Housed (Old Vic New Voices); The Silence of The Sea (Donmar).**

As Associate Movement Director, theatre includes: **In Time O' Strife, Black Watch (National Theatre of Scotland); The Curious Incident of the Dog in the Night-Time (National/West End).**

As Actor, theatre includes: **In Time O' Strife, Knives in Hens, Home Inverness (National Theatre of Scotland);**

Beautiful Burnout (Frantic Assembly/ National Theatre of Scotland); Dr Dee (ENO/Manchester International Festival); The Two Gentlemen of Verona (Royal & Derngate); (in)visible dancing, LOL, To the Bone (Protein Dance).

Glyn Pritchard (Monkey Father)

For the Royal Court: **Body Talk.**

Other theatre includes: **The Bee (Tokyo Metropolitan/tour); Blodeuwedd (Theatr Genedlaethol Cymru); The Dark Philosophers (National Theatre Wales); The Black Album, Ghetto, Fuente Ovejuna, Bartholomew Fair (National); The Bee, The Diver (Soho); Under Milkwood, Blue Remembered Hills, A Christmas Carol (Dukes, Lancaster); King Lear (Young Vic); Othello (RSC); The Marriage of Figaro (Royal Exchange, Manchester); A Family Affair (Arcola).**

Television includes: **Inspector George Gently, Critical, Harriet's Army, Law & Order: UK, Babylon, Hinterland, Stella, Casualty, The Indian Doctor, Pobol Y Cwm, Brookside, Oh Na! Y Morgans, Death of a Son, Famous Five, Coronation Street, A Mind To Kill.**

Film includes: **Hunky Dory, Weekenders, Butterflies.**

Katy Rudd (Associate Director)

As Director, theatre includes: **Juicy & Delicious, Beasts of Southern Wild (National); A Curious Night at the Theatre (West End); I'm Really Glad We Had That Chat (Arcola); Henna Night (Edinburgh International Festival); The Butterfly (Salisbury Playhouse); Narcissus (Edge, Leeds); The 24 Hour Plays: New Voices (Old Vic); Hippolytus (Stage@Leeds); Shafted (NCM Museum).**

As Associate Director, theatre includes: **The Curious Incident of the Dog in the Night-Time (National/West End/ Broadway/tour).**

As Staff Director, theatre includes: **Damned by Despair (National).**

As Assistant Director, theatre includes: **Mathematics of the Heart (503); 24 Hour Plays Gala Performance, The Playboy of the Western World (Old Vic); Bed & Sofa (Finborough); The Constant Wife, The Family Cookbook (Salisbury); Into the Woods (Regent's Park Open Air).**

John Tiffany (Director)

For the Royal Court: **Hope, The Pass, Let the Right One In (& National Theatre of Scotland/St Ann's, New York).**

Other theatre includes: **The Ambassador (Brooklyn Academy of Music); Once (West End/Broadway/New York Theatre Workshop); The Glass Menagerie (Broadway/American Repertory); Enquirer (co-director), Macbeth, Peter Pan, The House of Bernarda Alba, Transform Caithness: Hunter, Be Near Me, Nobody Will Ever Forgive Us, The Bacchae, Black Watch, Elizabeth Gordon Quinn, Home: Glasgow (National Theatre of Scotland); If Destroyed True (& Dundee Rep), Mercury Fur, The Straits, Helmet (Paines Plough); Gagarin Way, Passing Places (Traverse).**

Awards Include: **Tony, Lortell, Drama Desk Awards (Once); Laurence Olivier Award for Best Director, Critics Circle Award for Best Director, South Bank Show Award (Black Watch).**

John is an Associate Director at the Royal Court. From 2010 to 2011 he was a Radcliffe Fellow at Harvard University.

Dwane Walcott (Handsome Waltzer Boy)

Theatre includes: **Venice Preserv'd (The Spectator's Guild); Coriolanus (Donmar); Titus Andronicus, A Mad World, My Masters, Candide (RSC); Damned by Despair (National); Romeo & Juliet (Stafford Festival Shakespeare); Torque (Bush); Blood, Sweat & Fears (Extant); The Fiddler, Life on the Stairs (Faith Drama).**

Television includes: **Tut, Doctors.**

Film includes: **Oneway Film, Flashmob.**

Jason Watkins (Mr Twit)

For the Royal Court: **Boy Gets Girl, Man of Mode, The Libertine (& Out of Joint), King Lear, Rafts & Dreams.**

Other theatre includes: **Strange Interlude, Our Class, Landscape with Weapon, Inadmissible Evidence (National); Farewell to the Theatre, After Darwin (Hampstead); The Late Henry Moss, A Midsummer Night's Dream (Almeida) A Laughing Matter, She Stoops to Conquer (National/Out of Joint); A Servant to Two Masters (RSC/West End); My Night With Reg, Bedroom Farce, Kafka's Dick, Filumena, Blue Heart (West End); Kissing the Pope, The Plantagenets, The Plain Dealer (RSC); Habeus Corpus (Donmar); The Dumb Waiter, Pinter Sketches (Oxford Playhouse); One Flea Spare, Keyboard Skills (Bush); A Handful of Dust (Cambridge Touring).**

Television includes: **The Lost Honour of Christopher Jefferies, W1A, The Hollow Crown, Trollied, Atlantis, Our Zoo, Dr Who, Psychoville, The Wrong Mans, Call the Midwife, Poirot, Being Human, Miranda, Life on Mars, Miss Austen Regrets, Vivian Vyle, Man in a Box, May Contain Nuts, Housewife 49, Larkrise to Candleford, Little Crackers, Funland, Wired, Sex Traffic, Twenty Twelve, The Hour, Five Days, Little Dorrit, Prisoners' Wives, Dirk Gently, Victoria Wood Christmas Special, Murderland, Lewis, Silent Witness: Conviction, Elizabeth – The Virgin Queen, All About George, The Russian Bride, The Last Detective, Hotel Babylon, Bodies, Fear of Fanny, The Thick of it, Sex 'n' Death, The History of Mr Polly, Bostocks Cup, Between the Lines, The Buddha of Suburbia.**

Film includes: **Nativity! 1, 2 & 3, Lost Christmas, Wild Child, The Golden Compass, Sixty Six Confetti, Tomorrow Never Dies, Bridget Jones: The Edge of Reason, Sabotage, Circus, Eugene Onegin, High Hopes, Split Second.**

Radio Includes: **Under My Bed, Dissolution, Be Mine, Arcadia, Sunk, Our Mutual Friend, The Airship, Life After Scandal.**

Awards include: **Helen Hayes Award for Best Actor (A Servant to Two Masters); Olivier Nomination for Best Supporting Actor (A Servant to Two Masters).**

JERWOOD THEATRE
UPSTAIRS

10 Apr - 16 May
Who Cares
by Michael Wynne

In the run up to the General Election the NHS is emerging as the key issue in the party political agenda. The Royal Court responds to the debate by staging a new verbatim play.

3 Jun - 11 Jul
Violence and Son
by Gary Owen

An intimate new play about what parents pass on and trying to do the right thing.

18 Jul - 25 Jul
Primetime

A series of new short plays written by primary school children aged eight to 11.

Primetime is supported by John Lyon's Charity, The Mercers' Company, John Thaw Foundation, and The Austin and Hope Pilkington Trust.

JERWOOD THEATRE
DOWNSTAIRS

11 Jun - 18 Jul
hang
written and directed by
debbie tucker green

A shattering new play about an unspeakable decision.

WEST END

Until 25 Apr
The Nether
by Jennifer Haley

★ ★ ★ ★ ★
**"Mind-bending...
Ingenious"**
The Times

DUKE OF YORK'S THEATRE

A Headlong and Royal Court Theatre co-production. Presented by Sonia Friedman Productions and Scott M Delman in association with Tulchin Bartner Productions, Lee Dean & Charles Diamond, 1001 Nights, JFL Theatricals/GHF Productions, Scott + Brian Zellinger / James Lefkowitz.

ON TOUR

14 May – 4 Jul
Constellations
by Nick Payne

★ ★ ★ ★ ★
"Extraordinary. Dazzling."
Independent

NEW VICTORIA THEATRE (WOKING), LIVERPOOL PLAYHOUSE, BRISTOL OLD VIC, NUFFIELD THEATRE (SOUTHAMPTON), THE LOWRY (SALFORD QUAYS), CAMBRIDGE ARTS THEATRE, RICHMOND THEATRE, THEATRE ROYAL BRIGHTON.

Constellations was first staged in 2012 as part of the Royal Court's Jerwood New Playwrights programme, supported by Jerwood Charitable Foundation.

2 – 7 Jun
Not I / Footfalls / Rockaby
by Samuel Beckett

★ ★ ★ ★ ★
"Stunning. Moving. Chilling."
Daily Telegraph

BARBICAN CENTRE

Presented by the Royal Court Theatre and Lisa Dwan in association with Cusack Projects Ltd.

020 7565 5000 (no booking fee)
royalcourttheatre.com

Follow us 🐦 royalcourt 📘 royalcourttheatre
Royal Court Theatre Sloane Square London, SW1W 8AS

Innovation partner
 Coutts ♛

 Supported using public funding by
**ARTS COUNCIL
ENGLAND**

THE ROYAL COURT THEATRE

The Royal Court Theatre is the writers' theatre. It is the leading force in world theatre for energetically cultivating writers – undiscovered, new, and established.

Through the writers the Royal Court is at the forefront of creating restless, alert, provocative theatre about now, inspiring audiences and influencing future writers. Through the writers the Royal Court strives to constantly reinvent the theatre ecology, creating theatre for everyone.

We invite and enable conversation and debate, allowing writers and their ideas to reach and resonate beyond the stage, and the public to share in the thinking.

Over 120,000 people visit the Royal Court in Sloane Square, London, each year and many thousands more see our work elsewhere through transfers to the West End and New York, national and international tours, residencies across London and site-specific work.

The Royal Court's extensive development activity encompasses a diverse range of writers and artists and includes an ongoing programme of writers' attachments, readings, workshops and playwriting groups. Twenty years of pioneering work around the world means the Royal Court has relationships with writers on every continent.

The Royal Court opens its doors to radical thinking and provocative discussion, and to the unheard voices and free thinkers that, through their writing, change our way of seeing.

Within the past sixty years, John Osborne, Arnold Wesker and Howard Brenton have all started their careers at the Court. Many others, including Caryl Churchill, Mark Ravenhill and Sarah Kane have followed. More recently, the theatre has found and fostered new writers such as Polly Stenham, Mike Bartlett, Bola Agbaje, Nick Payne and Rachel De-lahay and produced many iconic plays from Laura Wade's **Posh** to Bruce Norris' **Clybourne Park** and Jez Butterworth's **Jerusalem**. Royal Court plays from every decade are now performed on stage and taught in classrooms across the globe.

It is because of this commitment to the writer that we believe there is no more important theatre in the world than the Royal Court.

Supported using public funding by
ARTS COUNCIL ENGLAND

ROYAL COURT SUPPORTERS

The Royal Court is a registered charity and not-for-profit company. We need to raise £1.7 million every year in addition to our core grant from the Arts Council and our ticket income to achieve what we do.

We have significant and longstanding relationships with many generous organisations and individuals who provide vital support. Royal Court supporters enable us to remain the writers' theatre, find stories from everywhere and create theatre for everyone.

We can't do it without you.

INDIVIDUAL SUPPORTERS

Major Donors
Eric Abraham
Ray Barrell & Ursula Van Almsick
Cas Donald
Lydia & Manfred Gorvy
Richard & Marcia Grand
Jack & Linda Keenan
Adam Kenwright
Mandeep Manku
Miles Morland
Mr & Mrs Sandy Orr
NoraLee & Jon Sedmak
Deborah Shaw & Stephen Marquardt
Jan & Michael Topham
Monica B Voldstad

Mover-Shakers
Anonymous
Jordan Cook
Piers & Melanie Gibson
Duncan Matthews QC
Mr & Mrs Timothy D Proctor
Ian & Carol Sellars

Boundary-Breakers
Anonymous
Katie Bradford
David Harding
Madeleine Hodgkin
Roderick & Elizabeth Jack
Nicola Kerr
Philip & Joan Kingsley
Emma Marsh
Rachel Mason
Andrew & Ariana Rodger

Ground-Breakers
Anonymous
Moira Andreae
Mr & Mrs Simon Andrews
Nick Archdale
Elizabeth & Adam Bandeen
Michael Bennett
Sam & Rosie Berwick
Dr Kate Best
Christopher Bevan
Sarah & David Blomfield
Deborah Brett
Peter & Romey Brown
Joanna Buckenham
Clive & Helena Butler

Piers Butler
Sindy & Jonathan Caplan
Gavin & Lesley Casey
Sarah & Philippe Chappatte
Tim & Caroline Clark
Carole & Neville Conrad
Andrea & Anthony Coombs
Clyde Cooper
Ian & Caroline Cormack
Mr & Mrs Cross
Andrew & Amanda Cryer
Alison Davies
Roger & Alison De Haan
Matthew Dean
Sarah Denning
Polly Devlin OBE
Rob & Cherry Dickins
Denise & Randolph Dumas
Robyn Durie
Glenn & Phyllida Earle
Graham & Susanna Edwards
Mark & Sarah Evans
Sally & Giles Everist
Celeste & Peter Fenichel
Margy Fenwick
The Edwin Fox Foundation
Dominic & Claire Freemantle
Beverley Gee
Nick & Julie Gould
Lord & Lady Grabiner
Jill Hackel & Andrzej Zarzycki
Carol Hall
Maureen Harrison
Sam & Caroline Haubold
Mr & Mrs Gordon Holmes
Kate Hudspeth
Damien Hyland
Suzie & David Hyman
Amanda & Chris Jennings
Melanie J Johnson
Nicholas Jones
Susanne Kapoor
David P Kaskel
 & Christopher A Teano
Vincent & Amanda Keaveny
Peter & Maria Kellner
Steve Kingshott
Mr & Mrs Pawel Kisielewski
David & Sarah Kowitz
Daisy & Richard Littler
Kathryn Ludlow
Suzanne Mackie
Dr Ekaterina Malievskaia
 & George Goldsmith
Christopher Marek Rencki
Mr & Mrs Marsden

Mrs Janet Martin
Andrew McIver
David & Elizabeth Miles
Barbara Minto
Takehito Mitsui
Angelie Moledina
M. Murphy Altschuler
Peter & Maggie Murray-Smith
Ann & Gavin Neath CBE
Clive & Annie Norton
Kate O'Neill
Jonathan Och & Rita Halbright
Georgia Oetker
Adam Oliver-Watkins
Anatol Orient
Sir William & Lady Vanessa Patey
Andrea & Hilary Ponti
Annie & Preben Prebensen
Greg & Karen Reid
Paul & Gill Robinson
Daniel Romualdez
Sir Paul & Lady Ruddock
William & Hilary Russell
Sally & Anthony Salz
Bhags Sharma
Tom Siebens & Mimi Parsons
Andy Simpkin
Andrea Sinclair & Serge Kremer
Paul & Rita Skinner
Brian Smith
Saadi & Zeina Soudavar
The Ulrich Family
Constanze Von Unruh
Matthew & Sian Westerman
Mrs Alexandra Whiley
Anne-Marie Williams
Sir Robert & Lady Wilson
Katherine & Michael Yates

With thanks to our Friends, Stage-Taker, Ice-Breaker and Future Court members whose support we greatly appreciate.

Innovation partner

Supported using public funding by

ARTS COUNCIL ENGLAND

EMPLOYEES
THE ROYAL COURT & ENGLISH STAGE COMPANY

The Royal Court has been on the cutting edge of new drama for more than 50 years. Thanks to our members, we are able to undertake the vital support of writers and the development of their plays – work which is the lifeblood of the theatre.

In acknowledgement of their support, members are invited to venture beyond the stage door to share in the energy and creativity of Royal Court productions.

Please join us as a member to celebrate our shared ambition whilst helping to ensure our ongoing success.

We can't do it without you.

royalcourttheatre.com

To join as a Royal Court member from £250 a year, please contact:
Anna Sampson, Development Manager
annasampson@royalcourttheatre.com
020 7565 5049

ROALD DAHL'S
THE TWITS

Enda Walsh

Characters

MONKEY DAD
MONKEY DAUGHTER
MONKEY MAM
MONKEY SON
MR TWIT
MRS TWIT
TATTOOED FORTUNE-TELLER LADY
HANDSOME WALTZER BOY
YORKSHIRE TERRIER MAN

This text went to press before the end of rehearsals and so may differ slightly from the play as performed.

ACT ONE

There's a cage in the front of the stage – and crammed inside this cage is a family of flea-ridden, emaciated MONKEYS – *dressed in simple play clothes* (*like the children in* The Sound of Music).

MONKEY DAUGHTER *is working on something we can't see – as* MONKEY MAM *holds a little mirror redirecting moonlight to light her daughter's work – and* MONKEY SON *chews on his nails.*

From a small purse hanging around her neck – MONKEY DAUGHTER *takes out a large monkey's tooth.*

MONKEY SON *grimaces.*

MONKEY DAD *slowly turns and faces us.*

His eyes widen as he sees us for the very first time.

Channelling Richard Burton – he speaks in a Welsh accent. (*They are all Welsh.*)

MONKEY DAD (*whispers*). No one would have believed in the early years of the twenty-first century – that man could be so despicable to a monkey. Until this moment – my family and I have been incarcerated here in this terrible cage for... (*To his wife.*) How long have we been here?

MONKEY DAUGHTER. Ages.

MONKEY DAD. But how long, would you say?

MONKEY MAM. What sort of a question is that!?

MONKEY DAD. Around how long have we been here?

MONKEY DAUGHTER. How would we know? – We don't have any watches.

MONKEY MAM. Who wants to know anyway?

MONKEY DAD. I want to know!

3

MONKEY MAM. Don't you know?!

MONKEY DAD. Well obviously not!

MONKEY DAUGHTER. I was born in this cage.

MONKEY DAD. Excellent! – And how old are you?

MONKEY DAUGHTER. No idea – but I'm younger than he is.

MONKEY DAD (*to his son*). And you're what?

MONKEY SON. I'm starving!

MONKEY DAD. Right.

MONKEY SON. Completely starving! The last bit of food I had was a lick of a stick – and that was a whole three days ago now. I loved that stick, Mam.

MONKEY MAM. I know you did, love.

MONKEY SON. Proper loved it!

MONKEY MAM. I know.

MONKEY DAD (*to audience*). We've been here a long time, let's say – not for ever – but a significant amount of time.

MONKEY DAUGHTER. We've been here my whole life –

MONKEY DAD. That's right.

MONKEY DAUGHTER. – which some might say is significant.

MONKEY MAM. You are significant, dear, you are – and brilliant too!

MONKEY DAUGHTER. Thank you, Mam.

MONKEY MAM. I couldn't be prouder of the work you're constructing at this very moment...

MONKEY SON. And the musical composition I'm writing to accompany our escape into freedom, too, Mam.

MONKEY MAM. Oh absolutely, my little monkey-Mozart – and although I haven't heard one second of music spat from your tiny brain – I can already tell that it will be a glorious symphony.

4

MONKEY SON. Thank you for believing in me.

MONKEY MAM. Of course, poppet. Just think, my loved ones – soon we will be over that wall – we will be running to our freedom – setting up our own monkey house – sitting around a proper table having our own little monkey tea party.

MONKEY SON. 'Cause that's the dream, isn't it?

MONKEY MAM. That is the dream, son.

MONKEY DAD (*to audience*). No one would have believed in the early years of the twenty-first century that man could be so despicable…

MONKEY MAM. What are you doing – who are you talking to?!

MONKEY DAD. I'm explaining things.

MONKEY MAM. Yes but to who?!

MONKEY DAD. I'm not too sure yet.

MONKEY MAM. Well will you stop doing that – it's very creepy!

MONKEY DAD. I am speaking aloud and outwards so as to document this marvellous occasion that we're all about to witness!

MONKEY DAUGHTER. There won't be anything marvellous if I'm not allowed to concentrate on my work, family – now please… shush now!

A long pause.

MONKEY SON (*whispers*). Can anyone do this talking out, Dad?!

MONKEY DAD. Absolutely anyone can do it! It's a free country!

MONKEY MAM. Says the monkey in the cage.

MONKEY DAD. Speak what you feel, son… but speak that way.

MONKEY SON. Why's that?

MONKEY DAD. Added significance.

MONKEY SON. Oh.

MONKEY SON *turns out to the audience and he too speaks as Richard Burton –*

(*Acting terrified.*) No one would have believed in the early years of the twenty-first century – that man could be so despicable to a monkey. Until this moment – my family and I have been incarcerated here in this terrible cage – trapped in this putrid garden – forced often to stand on our monkey heads... by 'them'.

MONKEY DAD (*again as Richard*). By these ghastly people.

MONKEY SON. These hateful humans.

MONKEY DAD. These odious creatures.

MONKEY SON. These...? – Posh Gits.

MONKEY DAD. These – Vicious Twits.

MONKEY SON. Satisfying, isn't it?

MONKEY DAD. Yeah, very. Carry on then!

MONKEY MAM. Don't we have enough drama in our lives without narrating it all out?!

MONKEY SON (*sees audience*). Is something out there...?

MONKEY DAUGHTER. It's done! I've only gone and done it!

The MONKEY DAUGHTER *holds up a large, bizarre key.*

Fashioned from the bones of birds, the ear-hair of a monkey dad – the tooth of a monkey brother – and bound together by a monkey mam's spit, snot –

MONKEY MAM. – and eye-bogey.

MONKEY DAUGHTER. Twelve months in its construction and has freedom ever looked more beautiful than this key?

MONKEY DAD. Never!

MONKEY MAM. You did ever so well, love – now open that blasted door!

Holding her key, the MONKEY DAUGHTER *stretches out her hand through the bars and places the key in the lock.*

She suddenly sees us too and stops.

MONKEY DAUGHTER. Daddy?

MONKEY DAD. Yes, my love.

MONKEY DAUGHTER. What's out there in the semi-darkness?

A slight pause.

MONKEY SON. There is – 'something', isn't there.

MONKEY DAD. They are witnesses, kids. Witnesses to this great moment – that's who they are.

MONKEY MAM *now sees us.*

MONKEY MAM. Good Lord.

MONKEY DAD. Witnesses – to this great escape.

MONKEY DAUGHTER. Prepare to play your rubbish musical composition, brother!

She turns the key and we hear it loudly 'click'.

She slowly pushes the cage door open.

MONKEY SON *plays something vaguely musical on the bars of the cage.*

Their freedom won – and for a beautiful moment the family smile through happy tears.

MONKEY MAM (*to her daughter*). On your way, love.

MONKEY DAUGHTER *steps out of the cage.*

Suddenly, a loud car horn is heard blaring 'IT'S THE TWITS THE TWITS THE TWITS THE TWITS THE TWITS'.

MONKEY DAUGHTER *steps back into the cage – and* MONKEY DAD *slowly closes the cage door shut as his children and wife retreat and stand on their heads.*

The sound of a car skidding to a stop on a gravel driveway.

MONKEY DAD. Whoever you are out there… you should prepare yourselves. They're coming.

He is about to stand on his head –

They're here.

Blood-curdling screams meld with a wild raucous syncopated rhythm.

MR *and* MRS TWIT *appear with electrical cables.*

MONKEY DAUGHTER. The key, Daddy – the key!

MONKEY DAD *reaches out to retrieve the key but it is too late –*

MR TWIT. Don't even think about it!!

MR TWIT *grabs the key and eats it like it was a Tuc cracker.*

The TWITS *attach the cables to the cage – electrocuting the* MONKEYS *inside.*

The TWITS *screech hysterically like it's the funniest thing ever.*

They then walk towards a kitchen space – the decor, decayed and disgusting.

Silence and semi-stillness then.

MR *and* MRS TWIT *face one another – her holding her walking stick aloft.*

In this stillness we have a number of quiet moments when we can observe these beasts.

And what disgusting creatures they are. They are British eccentrics of the darkest, smelliest kind – filthy, hairy grotesqueries – crackling with the energy of rabid rats.

MRS TWIT *– smashes her walking stick into the floor.*

A new syncopated rhythm is heard – and so begins a daily routine – of cruel trickery.

MRS TWIT. Some lunch, Mr Twit?

MR TWIT. Why yes, Mrs Twit.

MR TWIT *pokes his wife in the eye. She staggers back, grabs a frying pan – and crashes it down on her husband's head. He hits the ground fast – and she walks over him.*

She takes a large saucepan from the wall. As she walks back towards the kitchen area (a small camping stove) she crashes the saucepan into MR TWIT's head.

She puts the saucepan on the stove, fills it with spaghetti and dark water.

Meanwhile MR TWIT *– lying on the floor – has spotted something. A fat frog. He grabs it with one hand – and raises it upwards like it were Excalibur.*

He taps his wife on the shoulder – she spins around. Hiding the frog, he offers his other hand to dance. She tentatively takes it.

He whisks her around and shoves the frog down the front of her blouse.

MRS TWIT *explodes into convulsions – the frog twisting her into a demented Morris dancer.* MR TWIT *watches her while scoffing a banana. He drops the skin on the floor.*

Unable to resist the pull of the banana skin's gravity – MRS TWIT *is dragged perilously towards it.*

MR TWIT *grabs a potato and a potato gun – and nonchalantly shoots potato pellets at his wife.*

Capoeira-style – she dodges them – but still she may be slain by the banana.

MR TWIT *grabs a Kodak Pocket Instamatic camera and takes a picture of his wife.*

FLASH!

Blinded (as we are) and the gyrating MRS TWIT *slips on the banana skin – and crashes onto her back with a CRUNCH!*

MR TWIT *deserves a tipple for that. Like James Bond – he saunters over to a little bar area and pulls himself a pint of bitter. He sees her walking stick beside him.*

He's got an idea.

MRS TWIT *meanwhile is upright. The dazed flattened frog falls from inside her skirt with a plop. It crawls offstage like a wounded soldier. She stares over at* MR TWIT*'s back.*

From a large tin of Hugtight Glue – MR TWIT *secretly starts gluing bits of wood to the end of her stick.*

MRS TWIT reaches into her eye socket and removes her glass eye.

She walks over to her husband and taps him on the shoulder. He stops his work and spins around.

Hiding the glass eye behind her back, she offers her other hand to dance. He tentatively takes it.

As they dance she pops her glass eye into his pint of bitter. She stops dancing and steps back from him.

All mock-sexy – she raises her skirt to show her revolting knees.

He'll need some Dutch courage to 'proceed'. He grabs his bitter and knocks it back. The glass eye catches in his throat.

As he chokes towards death – he tries to bang his back – first with his hand – and then with MRS TWIT*'s recently glued walking stick.*

Meanwhile MRS TWIT *– like a one-eyed Scarlett Johansson – saunters over to the bar area and finishes his pint of bitter.*

MR TWIT *– whipping himself like a horse – finally dislodges the glass eye. It fires out of his mouth – across the living room – and back into* MRS TWIT*'s eye socket.*

MR TWIT *walks over to his wife and hands her the walking stick. She goes to use it but it is too large. Terrified – she drops it – jumps away from it and begins to convulse with fear.*

MR TWIT *stands holding a wooden chair and the tin of Hugtight Glue.*

MRS TWIT *turns and grabs the large saucepan of spaghetti. She slams it down on the floor – and throws open a small trapdoor.*

She pulls out handfuls of worms and dirt and adds it to the spaghetti.

As MRS TWIT *cooks the worm spaghetti on the stove –* MR TWIT *is busy with the wooden chair and the glue.*

He turns around and offers her a seat. The chair is suddenly ridiculously huge. She can't get into it.

MRS TWIT *then sees her husband beginning to tower above her – on small stilts she can't see – as he eats the worm spaghetti.*

She's shrinking!

MRS TWIT. The Shrinks – The Dreaded Shrinks!! ENOUGH! ENOUGH! ENOOOOOOOOOOOOOOUGHHHH!

The playing suddenly stops – the MONKEYS *are thoroughly exhausted.*

MR TWIT*'s shrinking prank was a terrible joke too far. A worm wriggles from his mouth.*

They must turn their energies elsewhere.

Then suddenly an idea –

Let's have a garden party!!

MR TWIT. No.

MRS TWIT *twists his arm behind his back. She's about to tear it off.*

MRS TWIT. Let's have a garden party! We can invite those fairground folk.

MR TWIT. What a wonderful idea!

That raucous syncopated rhythm returns.

A small battered 1960s bubble caravan is being dragged and pushed on stage.

As the caravan inches on – a 'garden' forms around it – of large skeletal trees, thorn bush and refuse. Tatty bunting is tangled through the trees – adding to the menace.

Most importantly – and most disturbing of all – large magpies (dead-ish) seem to be glued to the branches – as are the trousers of small boys.

The owners of the caravan come into view.

The young man who drags the caravan – is a muscle-ripped Adonis – all tight T-shirt and turned-up jeans, big boots. Battered and worn by hard years – his demeanour is forever cowered.

He is the HANDSOME WALTZER BOY.

On one side of the caravan – pushing at the rear – is a heavily tattooed woman – her hair like a trampled nest on her head. A faded beauty – life has exhausted her.

She is the TATTOOED FORTUNE-TELLER LADY.

Pushing on the other side of the caravan is a gangly moustachioed old man in a pinstriped suit.

This is the YORKSHIRE TERRIER MAN.

They are all from Yorkshire.

The music fades but continues at a suitable level as the caravan stops – and the GUESTS *look around at this dreadful garden.*

TATTOOED FORTUNE-TELLER LADY. So this is the place, ya reckon?

HANDSOME WALTZER BOY. It certainly looks like it might be Buckinghamshire.

YORKSHIRE TERRIER MAN. Ooh I do hope so – I'm completely jiggered, me.

HANDSOME WALTZER BOY. I'm feeling a little tired meself.

YORKSHIRE TERRIER MAN. Ya did ever so well though – draggin' that caravan! Brilliant work!

HANDSOME WALTZER BOY. You too, pal.

TATTOOED FORTUNE-TELLER LADY. Those motorways are hellish and endless, aren't they?

HANDSOME WALTZER BOY. And not altogether welcoming of a caravan either.

TATTOOED FORTUNE-TELLER LADY. No – not at that speed.

YORKSHIRE TERRIER MAN. You know what these past eleven weeks of pushin' that caravan along the motorways of England have taught me though? – It's that we're alive!

TATTOOED FORTUNE-TELLER LADY. Alive with pain, I'll give ya that.

YORKSHIRE TERRIER MAN. Yeah but at least we're feelin' somethin', love.

TATTOOED FORTUNE-TELLER LADY. Yeah, pain.

HANDSOME WALTZER BOY. The thought of gettin' back our beloved fairground – has carried me these past eleven wa-wa-weeks!

YORKSHIRE TERRIER MAN. And me.

TATTOOED FORTUNE-TELLER LADY. Yeah me too.

HANDSOME WALTZER BOY. After today, just imagine it, friends! No more livin' under that flyover in Leeds – I know that much. I can see myself spinning folk as they scream, 'Faster! Faster!' on my waltzer carousel.

TATTOOED FORTUNE-TELLER LADY. And me showin' people their fortunes through a brand-new crystal ball.

YORKSHIRE TERRIER MAN. And me, friends – creating a new doggie-acrobatic show!

TATTOOED FORTUNE-TELLER LADY. After today those glory days of when we travelled and entertained the good people of England will be ours once again!

YORKSHIRE TERRIER MAN. Back on road!

A loud squawk – and the three of them turn and look at the tree. One of the magpies seems to be alive (just).

That's a cheery welcome!

HANDSOME WALTZER BOY. Hello there, Mr Magpie.

HANDSOME WALTZER BOY *and* YORKSHIRE TERRIER MAN. How's your wife and kids?

TATTOOED FORTUNE-TELLER LADY. Dead, by the looks of them.

Suddenly a light comes up on MR *and* MRS TWIT *with loudspeakers –*

MR TWIT. After all these years – a reunion!

TATTOOED FORTUNE-TELLER LADY. We got your invitation and here we are, Mr Twit!

MR TWIT. Well you're late!

MRS TWIT. We don't really like lateness!

YORKSHIRE TERRIER MAN. Well we're here now, Mrs Twit.

MRS TWIT. Yes you're here now!

HANDSOME WALTZER BOY. Thanks for havin' us!

MR TWIT. Oh we haven't had you yet!

MRS TWIT. But we will!!

They laugh their screeching laughs – drop their loudspeakers – and appear –

MR *and* MRS TWIT. SURPRISE!

MRS TWIT. Welcome welcome welcomewelcomewelcome welcomewelcomewelklwecglomnequomewelcomewelklwec glomnequo –

MRS TWIT *runs around plucking glued magpies off the branches and flinging them offstage as the 'welcomes' get more ridiculous.*

– welcomewelcomewelklwecglomnequomewelcomewelk lwecglomnequo –

Suddenly she's holding a tray of peculiar hors d'oeuvres –

Welcome to our garden party! Lovely to see you all after all these years of not seeing you! Finally seeing you all together – with us – like this – I wonder, Mr Twit, why we didn't invite these people years ago!

MR TWIT. Impossible to say, Mrs Twit!

MRS TWIT. Is it to do with the fact – that actually we hate people.

MR TWIT. That we detest people, you mean?!

MRS TWIT. That we find people generally, you know – aggravating.

MR TWIT. That they irritate us, you mean?!

MRS TWIT. That we find people wretched.

MR TWIT. THAT THEY DISGUST US!!

MRS TWIT. It probably has to do with all those things, Mr Twit! And yet here we are on this summer's day having a garden party for people who were once vaguely known to us!

HANDSOME WALTZER BOY (*about the hors d'oeuvres*). Sorry but what exactly are these…?

MRS TWIT (*pretending to stammer*). Wh-wh-wh-wh-wh – ex-zac-zac-zac lelele-de-de-de-de foo-foo-foo.

HANDSOME WALTZER BOY. What exactly is this food?!

MR TWIT. You learnt to talk?! He learnt to talk!

HANDSOME WALTZER BOY. It is food, right?

MRS TWIT. Oh I abhor waste, I do!

MR TWIT. She absolutely hates waste!

MRS TWIT. I HATE IT!

MRS TWIT *flirts with the* HANDSOME WALTZER BOY –

(*As Nigella Lawson.*) You can pulverise, roll into balls and deep-fry anything you like.

The HANDSOME WALTZER BOY *drags an impossibly long hair out of his mouth – with something very nasty on the end of it.*

MR TWIT. Ohhhhh it's just so lovely to see them back together like this?!!

MRS TWIT. It's delightful, isn't it?!

TATTOOED FORTUNE-TELLER LADY. We were very surprised to get your invitation, to be honest.

MR TWIT. And why's that?

YORKSHIRE TERRIER MAN (*about the* TATTOOED FORTUNE-TELLER LADY). Well last time you saw her – you stole the fairground off us.

MR TWIT. *Stole* a fairground off you?!

MRS TWIT. Stole a fairground?! Did you, Mr Twit, did you *steal* a fairground off these Yorkshire people?

YORKSHIRE TERRIER MAN. Well yeah ya did. We woke up one morning and the fairground was gone – completely stolen from under our noses.

MR TWIT. But did I? Did I actually *steal* it – Tattooed Fortune-Teller Lady – (*Whispers to her.*) is that what you told them, you naughty-naughty-girl?! That's not really the truth, is it?

HANDSOME WALTZER BOY. We loved that fairground.

MR TWIT (*and back to the others*). So we packed up that fairground – and brought that fairground back here to lovely Bucks! Oooooh the excitement!! I had this fantasy, you see, of running my very own fairground! All those rides and noises and terrifying screams – (*Screams for a very long time. Then stops.*) it seemed like the perfect hobby for a man of my class. I unbundled that fairground right here in this garden – and only then did I realise that to activate all that noise, all those rides, all that delicious screaming – I would need the one thing I absolutely hate the most – people.

HANDSOME WALTZER BOY. So that's why you're giving the fairground back to us then?

MR TWIT. Oh absolutely it is!

MRS TWIT. It's all yours, Handsome Waltzer Boy, Yorkshire Terrier Man and Tattooed Fortune-Teller Lady!

YORKSHIRE TERRIER MAN. Aye but where is it?

TATTOOED FORTUNE-TELLER LADY. We couldn't see it anywhere on the way in – d'ya have it close by?

MRS TWIT. Oh it's very close, yes.

TATTOOED FORTUNE-TELLER LADY. Oh we'll pick it up and get right on our way then!

MR TWIT. Moments from now a gentleman will arrive with your fairground on the back of a fleet of magnificent vehicles!

HANDSOME WALTZER BOY. Ooh excellent!

MRS TWIT. This gentleman was employed by us – at some expense – with the careful restoration of your wonderful fun machines.

YORKSHIRE TERRIER MAN. Bloomin' 'eck!

MR TWIT. This very day – he will enter the grounds of our estate – the sparkling fairground returneth – to you!

TATTOOED FORTUNE-TELLER LADY. Thank you, Mr Twit!

MR TWIT. Oh darling, just to see your little face – it's our pleasure, really!

MRS TWIT. Now by way of celebration, we have created a presentation to bask once again in the glory of the fair!

HANDSOME WALTZER BOY. What ya mean?

MRS TWIT. We have created – a show! Bring in the Muggle-Wumps!!

Somehow the monkey cage appears on stage – the MONKEYS *trapped inside.*

YORKSHIRE TERRIER MAN (*excited*). Monkeys!

HANDSOME WALTZER BOY. Oh I love monkeys, me – I love 'em!!

TATTOOED FORTUNE-TELLER LADY. A monkey show – fantastic!

HANDSOME WALTZER BOY. And in clothes too, love – even better!

The MONKEYS *are let out of their cage.*

MRS TWIT. Sit down, dear guests. Rest your tired bones and savour this magical recreation!

MR TWIT. Costumes costumes!!

Excited and the three GUESTS *seat themselves.*

MONKEY DAD *looks out to us –*

MONKEY DAD. Is there anything less funny in the world – than dressing up monkeys, tell me?

MONKEY SON. Are we going to be doing this talking out a lot, Dad?

MONKEY DAD. From this moment on – those faces out there – will witness the journey of our escape – from darkness – to triumph!

Secretly – MONKEY DAUGHTER *is removing some bird legs from the trees and putting them in her purse.*

The HANDSOME WALTZER BOY *pets her on the head.*

HANDSOME WALTZER BOY. What a cute little monkey this one is!

MONKEY DAUGHTER. You're pretty lush yourself.

HANDSOME WALTZER BOY. A *talking* monkey!! Flippin' 'eck!! Can this day get any better?!

TATTOOED FORTUNE-TELLER LADY. Are they actual monkeys, Mr Twit?

MR TWIT. Well many years ago… (*Grabbing the* MONKEY DAD *and* MAM *by the scruff of the neck.*) I saw these two monkeys joyfully performing in a Welsh circus. Ooh I just had to 'ave 'em! Nothing fulfils an animal more than rigorous continuous instruction, ya know.

YORKSHIRE TERRIER MAN. And love. Animals do have to be loved also.

MR TWIT. Like Baxter, you mean?

YORKSHIRE TERRIER MAN. Aye, Baxter – I loved that dog like I loved our fairground, didn't I, love?

TATTOOED FORTUNE-TELLER LADY. Yeah.

MR TWIT. Well wouldn't it be nice to peel back the years – to see once again the joy of that fairground – to relive your sweet love affair with Baxter!

YORKSHIRE TERRIER MAN. Well yes it would be lovely to be back in that world!

MRS TWIT (*applauding*). Excellent answer!!

MR TWIT. Then let us see again – YOUR FINEST DAY!

A sudden lighting change as a banner unfurls reading – 'YORKSHIRE TERRIER BRILLIANCE – TRICKS AND RACING. 4 Tokens'.

The sound of a carousel playing a medley of various overtures throughout – it is unhinged and terrifying.

The MONKEYS *perform a little play.*

MONKEY DAD. He woke in his little caravan to the sounds of the fairground outside. The air charged with anticipation – the good people of Great Missenden filling their pockets with money to spend.

MONKEY MAM. He woke as he did every morning – with thoughts of his beloved Baxter and what tricks and extraordinary agility that dog would display to the fine people of Great Missenden!

MONKEY DAD. The caravan door open –

MONKEY MAM. – he stepped outside.

MONKEY DAD. And how he loved Baxter – and how Baxter loved him. He hung on his words like those words were constructed from sausage.

MONKEY SON. It is Friday the twenty-fourth of May – and what I feel in my Yorkshire bones – is an expectation of a significant happenin' about to happen! Do you feel that too, Baxter?

MONKEY DAUGHTER. I do, Yorkshire Terrier Man – though unfortunately I can only communicate this understandin' by tappin' my paw on the ground – like so.

MONKEY SON. Good boy. Now by way of rehearsal – Begin, Baxter – Begin!

MONKEY DAUGHTER *does an agility course – the usual doggie-acrobatic stuff.*

MONKEY DAD. In rehearsal that morning – the dog was lithe like a snake – had the quick responses of a snapped elastic band.

MONKEY MAM. And as they rehearsed – and as the good people of Great Missenden parted with their money and awaited this athletic presentation – two titans sat in their Chrysler Avenger –

The TWITS *are getting excited. During the below –* MR *and* MRS TWIT *costume* MONKEY DAD *and* MAM *as themselves.*

They sat there sketching.

MONKEY DAD. Scheming. Mixing.

MONKEY MAM. Designing the Downfall of the Yorkshire Terrier Man and his dearest Baxter!

MONKEY DAD (*as* MR TWIT). Let us begin, Mrs Twit.

MONKEY MAM (*as* MRS TWIT). Yes, Mr Twit.

MR TWIT (*ecstatic*). Very good very good!!

The GUESTS (*especially the* YORKSHIRE TERRIER MAN) *are suddenly on edge.*

MONKEY SON. A little brekkie before your performance, Baxter?

MONKEY DAUGHTER. Oh yes please, master!

MONKEY SON. Let us return then to our caravan where I can prepare summat.

MONKEY MAM (*as* MRS TWIT). Beg your pardon, kind sir – but I have temporarily lost the use of my eyes – and my legs – and am unable to find my seat for yours and Baxter's performance.

MONKEY SON. Amuse yourself and stay awhile in this caravan, Baxter, while I tend to this smelly old lady – by draggin' her to her allotted seat.

MONKEY SON *drags* MONKEY MAM *– with some effort.*

MONKEY DAD *holds a bowl of steaming mush and approaches the* MONKEY DAUGHTER *– like a spider.*

MONKEY DAUGHTER. What delicious concoction is this – strange stranger, who I do not yet know?

MONKEY DAD (*as* MR TWIT). Eat away, Baxter, and allow this steaming mush to enhance your already spectacular performance!

MONKEY DAUGHTER. Bein' a dog – I have yet to evolve my
critical faculties to steer me away from any jeopardy! And
anyway – that's food in there! And I love food! I can't wait
to get me chops around it!!

MONKEY DAUGHTER eats the food.

A sudden immediate jolt of energy courses through her body.

MONKEY SON. The crowd awaits, Baxter! Let's begin!

*The crowd is heard cheering – the appropriate music is
played and* MONKEY SON *and* MONKEY DAUGHTER
*snap into an absurd movement – showing a crazed (foaming-
at-the-mouth) Baxter and the* YORKSHIRE TERRIER
MAN*'s failing attempts to control his delirious doggie.*

MONKEY MAM. And it was like the energy of a boy band
mixing with wasps and flies and fizz – it was like all of this
fired through the body of a Yorkshire terrier!

MONKEY DAD. And where before was focus and power –
now was just violent chaos. As he wrestled with his frenzied
doggie – his dark future exploded in his brain! His life – and
Baxter's life – was finished – consigned to glorious –
FAILURE!!

A gunshot noise as MONKEY SON *'shoots'* MONKEY
DAUGHTER *– twice.*

'Baxter' drops dead.

The lights go up with MR *and* MRS TWIT *applauding –*

MR TWIT. I think that was a true impersonation of events!

MRS TWIT. A near duplication, Mr Twit!! Naughty,
Muggle-Wumps!

YORKSHIRE TERRIER MAN. You poisoned Baxter and
turned him against me!? Is this story the truth!?

MRS TWIT. Oh let's leave those details in the past...!

YORKSHIRE TERRIER MAN. But I don't understand – was it
really you that made me shoot my own dog or not, Mr
Twit?!!

MR TWIT *takes him by the collar and has a quiet word –*

MR TWIT. You don't want to anger me – disappoint your friends – and risk losing your returning fairground, do you, Yorkshire *Non*-Terrier Man?

A slight pause.

YORKSHIRE TERRIER MAN. No of course not.

MR TWIT. Good boy.

The YORKSHIRE TERRIER MAN *walks back to his friends.*

TATTOOED FORTUNE-TELLER LADY. Are you all right, pal?

YORKSHIRE TERRIER MAN. Yeah.

TATTOOED FORTUNE-TELLER LADY. Was that story true? It were them who poisoned Baxter?

YORKSHIRE TERRIER MAN. Don't worry about it, love – it's all in the past now – leave it be.

A loud telephone ringing noise is heard. Attached to the tree is the telephone. MR TWIT *goes to it and answers it.*

MR TWIT. Oh what terrible news!

He slams down the phone. Suddenly he has a shotgun.

MRS TWIT. What is it, Mr Twit?

MR TWIT. It seems the fleet of vehicles in which the fairground is returning – has been disrupted by the weekend traffic of 'happy families travelling in their cars'.

MRS TWIT. Oh how disgusting and unfortunate.

MR TWIT (*loading his gun*). You'll have to rest your weary bones, I'm afraid, until the fairground arrives.

TATTOOED FORTUNE-TELLER LADY. And when might that be?

MR TWIT. Oh tomorrow morning at the very latest!

HANDSOME WALTZER BOY. A good night's sleep would be most welcome and another day waitin' won't hurt, hey, love?

TATTOOED FORTUNE-TELLER LADY (*distant*). Yeah right.

MONKEY DAUGHTER pulls ear-hair out of her brother's ear.

MONKEY SON. AHHHHHHHHHHHHHHHHHHHHHHHHH!

She places the hair in her purse.

'The Floral Dance' plays loudly.

The GUESTS are led back into their bubble caravan by MRS TWIT.

MRS TWIT. Night night, sweet friends!

The MONKEYS are forced back into their cage by MR TWIT –

MR TWIT. On your heads – on your heads!

The MONKEYS get on their heads – MR TWIT walks towards his house.

MR *and* MRS TWIT *step back into their kitchen.*

They face each other – and a moment's silence and contentment then.

What a wonderful day, that was.

MRS TWIT. Yes, Mr Twit. Glorious.

Suddenly MRS TWIT pokes her husband in the eye. He drops to his knees and looks back up at her –

MR TWIT. The Shrinks – the Shrinks!

MRS TWIT. You're on your knees, you stupid Twit!

She pulls him back up by the hair –

The syncopated music resumes.

MR TWIT *immediately grabs a frying pan – and crashes it down on his wife's head. She hits the ground hard. He walks over her.*

The light comes down on them as they continue to torture each other in the usual manner.

The light cross-fades into a new setting.

Movement here where we see the three Yorkshire GUESTS
spending time in the garden – where we see MR TWIT
typing a script on an old typewriter – where MRS TWIT
*removes more magpies from the tree and applies more
Hugtight Glue to the branches.*

*Throughout the scene – leaves begin to fall as we enter
autumn.*

The bubble caravan opens and we see the GUESTS *inside
their cramped capsule.*

*From a small table – they're eating bird pie – all spiky legs
and beaks.*

HANDSOME WALTZER BOY. Try as I might – I've yet to
develop a liking for bird pie.

YORKSHIRE TERRIER MAN. I've eaten all manner of pies,
me – and these pies are a very acquired taste.

HANDSOME WALTZER BOY. Cooking is not one of Mrs
Twit's skills, is it?

YORKSHIRE TERRIER MAN. She does serve the bird pies
with real enthusiasm, mind you.

HANDSOME WALTZER BOY. Oh she does yeah.

YORKSHIRE TERRIER MAN. It'd be very rude not be
appreciative really.

The TATTOOED FORTUNE-TELLER LADY *has been
quiet and the* HANDSOME WALTZER BOY *has noticed.*

HANDSOME WALTZER BOY. You all right, flower?

TATTOOED FORTUNE-TELLER LADY. Yeah of course.

HANDSOME WALTZER BOY. You've been a little quiet is all.

TATTOOED FORTUNE-TELLER LADY. No I'm fine – just
still thinkin' about stuff.

YORKSHIRE TERRIER MAN. About what stuff? – What is it?

TATTOOED FORTUNE-TELLER LADY. Well way back in
the summer did Mr and Mrs Twit not take a little too much
enjoyment from that story of Baxter's death?

HANDSOME WALTZER BOY. We spoke about this before – it weren't them – but them disgusting and horrible monkeys havin' all the fun!

TATTOOED FORTUNE-TELLER LADY. But the monkeys were taught to speak and read and memorise scripted words!

HANDSOME WALTZER BOY. Any teasing was from them chimps alone!

TATTOOED FORTUNE-TELLER LADY. But it were the Twits who poisoned Baxter!

HANDSOME WALTZER BOY. Look, I still say it – the Twits poisoned Baxter – and they stole what was once ours, yeah – but all is forgiven with the promise of our fairground returned to us!

TATTOOED FORTUNE-TELLER LADY. But it's been *eight* weeks we've been sat here in the garden! Look, we made a mistake, friends – we need to leave!

YORKSHIRE TERRIER MAN. Don't be talkin' like that!

TATTOOED FORTUNE-TELLER LADY. But it's useless!!

YORKSHIRE TERRIER MAN. I'm not ready to lose faith! Years of living under that flyover in Leeds – I'm not going back to that place, love! I can only have trust for Mr and Mrs Twit – I know how that sounds – but it's all I have! We're holding hope in our hands – and that hope will one day turn in to a new little puppy that I'll buy to replace sweet Baxter. A puppy – that I will raise and love – who will learn the wonders of doggie-acrobatics and perform nationwide in our beloved fairground! We must keep believing in the dream.

TATTOOED FORTUNE-TELLER LADY. But...

YORKSHIRE TERRIER MAN. Enough!

Then suddenly through the loudspeaker –

MR TWIT. HAPPY HALLOWEEN!!!!

Suddenly lights up big on MR *and* MRS TWIT *costumed as a very happy elderly suburban couple.* MRS TWIT *in a rocking chair,* MR TWIT – *holding his shotgun – stands behind her. The* MONKEYS *grouped around them.*

They start to sing 'There's No One Quite Like Grandma'. All the MONKEYS *sing the first chorus,* MONKEY SON *sings the first verse, after which –*

MRS TWIT. Absolutely!

MONKEY DAUGHTER sings the second verse, and all the MONKEYS *join in on the chorus.*

MRS TWIT *hands the* YORKSHIRE TERRIER MAN *a song sheet, who then sings the next verse, before everyone joins in sharing the rest of the song.*

The music continuing –

It was me all this time!! How awfully nice to see you on this hallowed evening – isn't it nice, Mr Twit?!

MR TWIT. It's positively wonderful to see them on this Hallows' Eve, Mrs Twit. And have you been preparing a Hallowe'en feast for us to feed on?

MRS TWIT. Have you been making fireworks whose explosion will speckle the black sky with sparkle?

MR TWIT. Have you laced our Hallowe'en sweets with needles and pins?! Do you plan to speckle the sky with Mr and Mrs Twit – is that your plan?! Is it?! Is it?!!

MRS TWIT. What have you been doing inside that caravan of yours?!

HANDSOME WALTZER BOY. Just waiting for…

MRS TWIT. Ju-ju-ju wa-wa-wa-wa fo-fo-fo…

HANDSOME WALTZER BOY. Just waiting for news about our fairground.

MR TWIT. You learnt to talk. He learnt to talk.

YORKSHIRE TERRIER MAN. We wondered whether there was any word from this man returning our fairground?

TATTOOED FORTUNE-TELLER LADY. It's been two months now!

MRS TWIT. The difficulty of transporting a lovingly refurbished fairground is something we've only been made aware of, isn't that right, Mr Twit?

MR TWIT. The British roads being so hazardous these days – it has sadly slowed the fairground's delivery.

MRS TWIT. It is however – very very very very near.

HANDSOME WALTZER BOY. Well that's great news!

YORKSHIRE TERRIER MAN. Brilliant!

MRS TWIT. Because of the absence of any Hallowe'en party – we'll have to create our own fireworks! Muggle-Wumps!

The MONKEYS *step forward.*

(*To the* GUESTS.) Be seated, dear guests.

The three GUESTS *sit on the branches of the trees –* MRS TWIT *snapping some magpies off the branches and throwing them on the ground.*

MONKEY DAUGHTER *immediately falls on her stomach – and commando-style – slowly crawls across the ground snapping the beaks off those dead birds.*

She retches up some bile and begins to stick the beaks to her primitive key.

She stands and conceals the key in her purse. She then sees us –

MONKEY DAUGHTER. All right?

A banner unfurls reading – 'THE ROCK 'N' ROLL CAROUSEL WALTZER – TEARS AND SCREAMS! 4 Tokens'.

HANDSOME WALTZER BOY (*to the* MONKEY DAUGHTER). So what's going on here? I'm warnin' you ch-cheeky monkeys – you better behave yourselves!

MONKEY DAUGHTER. I need to borrow your hat.

She steals his hat and races off with it.

MR TWIT. Oh it's a wonderful charming English fairground, isn't it? – And you love it so – don't you, you Handsome Waltzer Boy?

HANDSOME WALTZER BOY. Yeah, of course – we all love it – it's the most important thing in all our lives – always has been.

MRS TWIT (*looking at the* TATTOOED FORTUNE-TELLER LADY). Oh how sweet.

MR TWIT. Well wouldn't it be nice to peel back the years – to hear again that deafening music –

MRS TWIT. As you spin those little cars on your waltzer carousel –

MR TWIT. To relive – once again – your sweet love affair with that pretty girl in Great Missenden.

HANDSOME WALTZER BOY (*to the* MONKEY DAUGHTER). Don't you dare play me!!

MR TWIT. Then let us see again – YOUR FINEST DAY!

A sudden lighting change – and again the terrifying sound of a carousel playing a medley of various overtures throughout the MONKEYS' *little play.*

MONKEY DAD. He woke in his little caravan to the sounds of the fairground outside – the air charged with anticipation – the good people of Great Missenden filling their pockets with money to spend.

MONKEY MAM. He woke as he did every morning – with thoughts of his magnificent coolness – and whose girlish heart would he melt today – in the little town of Great Missenden?!

MONKEY DAD. The caravan door open –

MONKEY MAM. He stepped outside –

MONKEY DAUGHTER (*as the* HANDSOME WALTZER BOY). Great Missenden – EE BY GUM!

MONKEY DAD. The name of that town shot through his body like a firecracker! And like a wooden spaceship bedecked in coloured light bulbs – his waltzer carousel with its spinning cars – rose in front of him –

MONKEY MAM. And at the waltzer carousel's centre – his little cabin in which the waltzer boy now planned.

MONKEY DAUGHTER. It is Friday the twenty-fourth of May – and what my brain has just remembered is that we have decamped our beloved fairground to *Great Missenden*! *Great Missenden* – only the home of the prettiest girls in the whole of England! Oh my God!

MONKEY SON (*as the Pretty Girl*). And as us pretty girls paraded around town – a competition had started to see which girl would enter the waltzer cabin this afternoon. For generations of fantastically cool waltzer boys have melted hearts inside waltzer cabins – speaking glorious words of romantic poetry! And it will be my heart! It will be me!!

MONKEY DAUGHTER. And although this magnificent body of mine is blessed with the pa-power of Hercules and the grace of Darcey Bussell – for years when faced by pretty girls – it is my own va-voice which chews the air into a tortured na-na-noise. So as I have done many times before – I must prepare my waltzer carousel to scream loud pop music above my stammering and save me from what would be an appalling scene of public humiliation! To work then!

MONKEY DAD. And as he prepared his carousel to drown out his stammering poetry – and as the pretty girls of Great Missenden fought with one another for this fairytale romance – two titans sat in their Chrysler Avenger.

During the below, MR *and* MRS TWIT *costume* MONKEY MAM *and* DAD *as themselves*.

MONKEY MAM. They sat there sketching.

MONKEY DAD. Scheming. Mixing.

MONKEY MAM. Designing the Downfall of the Handsome Waltzer Boy and his wo-words!

TATTOOED FORTUNE-TELLER LADY. Oh God no.

The TWITS *are laughing* –

MONKEY DAD (*as* MR TWIT). Let us begin, Mrs Twit.

MONKEY MAM (*as* MRS TWIT). Yes, Mr Twit.

MRS TWIT. Very good – very good!

MONKEY DAUGHTER. Right then! I can be confident that this waltzer carousel will drown out my stammering poetry and fill the universe with loud pop music instead.

Excellent! The afternoon approaches – and so too my ever so pretty companion!

MONKEY DAUGHTER *deodorises herself (including her mouth) and adopts a debonair pose.*

From a distance MONKEY SON *triumphant.*

Suddenly MONKEY DAD *and* MAM *are in front of him –*

MONKEY DAD (*as* MR TWIT). Are you the prettiest girl in Great Missenden, young voluptuous lady?

MONKEY SON. Indeed I am, smelly disgusting old man. It is me who will sit with the Handsome Waltzer Boy while listening to his delightful poetry.

MONKEY MAM (*as* MRS TWIT). Then let us present you with this lover's pendant.

MONKEY SON. What sort of a lover's pendant is this, you creepy old fish?

She places the pendant around his neck.

MONKEY DAD. Well what it *isn't* – is a powerful device which wirelessly cuts the flow of electricity to any nearby waltzer carousels – operated from this hand-held instrument I have right here – it is not that.

MONKEY DAUGHTER. The time has come for some heart-breaking!

The MONKEY DAUGHTER *pivots and faces the* MONKEY SON *in the waltzer cabin.*

MONKEY SON. So this is what the inside of a waltzer carousel cabin looks like with its multitude of levers, buttons and electrical equipment.

MONKEY DAUGHTER *smoulders and purrs with coolness.*

Is this really the Centre of Enchantment? Is it true – you very attractive waltzer boy – that you speak words of romantic poetry like an extremely cool vicar?

MONKEY DAUGHTER. Why yes.

A slight pause.

MONKEY SON. Before I explode in girlish excitement – speak those glorious words to me then!

MONKEY DAUGHTER. One second, lo-love.

The MONKEY DAUGHTER *pulls a lever and the carousel music rises in volume.*

Gesturing like Rudolph Valentino she begins the poetry recital – the 'prettiest girl' unable to hear the terrible stammering.

As the MONKEY DAUGHTER *acts this out – the* HANDSOME WALTZER BOY *walks slowly into the light and faces his 'old self'.*

The MONKEY DAD *presses his device and the carousel music completely cuts – and then –*

…ta-ta-ta-ta-take my heart… And with it be-be-be-be gen-gen-gen-gen-gen-gen… (*'He' realises that he can be heard.*) Tle.

HANDSOME WALTZER BOY. Ta-ta-take ma-ma-ma-ma-my heart and be-be-be-be-be ge-ge-ge… gen-gentle. B-be gentle.

The HANDSOME WALTZER BOY*'s head drops – and it's like he's back in that moment.*

The MONKEYS *are devastated for him.*

MRS TWIT *pokes the* MONKEY SON –

MRS TWIT. It's your line, come on! Come on!!

Reluctantly, MONKEY SON *gets back into character.*

MONKEY SON. Is this some joke!?

MONKEY MAM. And that's when it starts.

MONKEY SON (*beginning to laugh*). I thought you were supposed to be fantastically cool!

MONKEY DAD. The laughter begins.

MONKEY SON. Did you hear how he talks, everyone?! Did you hear his stupid stammering voice?!!

During the below – laughter mixes with increasingly chaotic carousel music.

MONKEY DAD. And the good people of Great Missenden turned slowly to the silent waltzer carousel.

The HANDSOME WALTZER BOY *is alone in the light.*

MONKEY MAM. It lay dead and still – heavy with the humiliation of a boy – a beautiful hunk of a boy whose words crash in the company of pretty girls. The boy stood at the centre of the waltzer that last time – his dark future exploded in his brain – his life finished – consigned to glorious – FA-FA-FAILURE!!

The music/noise explodes and a moment of silence.

The HANDSOME WALTZER BOY *cries quietly.*

Suddenly he grabs the MONKEY DAUGHTER *by the throat and starts strangling her.*

HANDSOME WALTZER BOY. Why are you doing this to us?! Did you write this blasted script…!?

MONKEY DAUGHTER *(strangled)*. NO OF COURSE NOT! Monkeys can't type… *(Slight pause.)* that well! We're only badly trained actors!! They're making us do it!

Shattered and he drops his hands from her throat.

The lights go up on MR *and* MRS TWIT *applauding –*

MR TWIT. I think that was a true impersonation of events!

MRS TWIT. A near reproduction, Mr Twit! Very naughty Muggle-Wumps!

A loud telephone ringing noise is heard. MR TWIT *goes to the telephone and answers it.*

MR TWIT. Oh what wonderful news!

He slams down the phone. Suddenly he has a shotgun.

Tomorrow morning –

MRS TWIT. Yes yes yes yes yes?

MR TWIT. – the fairground returneth!

MRS TWIT *applauds enthusiastically.*

YORKSHIRE TERRIER MAN (*to* HANDSOME WALTZER BOY). Well that's good news, isn't it, son?

HANDSOME WALTZER BOY. I suppose.

TATTOOED FORTUNE-TELLER LADY (*to* MR TWIT). You're a liar! And it were you two who tricked my friends that final day – my God, why did we come here!?

Dragging her to one side –

MR TWIT. Quiet, you!

TATTOOED FORTUNE-TELLER LADY. That fairground's never coming back – why don't you just put us out of our misery!

MR TWIT. If you're not quiet – I will tell them about your significant role in losing their precious fairground – d'you understand?! It was never *stolen*!

TATTOOED FORTUNE-TELLER LADY. I want to leave!

MR TWIT (*as* MONKEY DAD). She woke in her little caravan to the sounds of the fairground outside – the air charged with anticipation…

TATTOOED FORTUNE-TELLER LADY. Stop it!

MR TWIT. Tell her story, Mrs Twit!

MRS TWIT (*as* MONKEY MAM). She sat as she did every morning with time at her fingertips – and what tantalising glimpses into the future would she and her crystal ball give to the good people of Great Missenden…

TATTOOED FORTUNE-TELLER LADY. Please stop…!

YORKSHIRE TERRIER MAN. What's happening…?

The YORKSHIRE TERRIER MAN *goes towards her and* MR TWIT.

Is something the matter, love? Some problem, maybe?

A slight pause.

MR TWIT. A problem? Is there a problem, Tattooed Fortune-Teller Lady?

A slight pause.

TATTOOED FORTUNE-TELLER LADY (*to* YORKSHIRE TERRIER MAN). No, everything's fine.

YORKSHIRE TERRIER MAN. You're sure?

TATTOOED FORTUNE-TELLER LADY. Yeah.

MR TWIT. Excellent answer.

MONKEY DAUGHTER. I can't do this any more, Mr Twit! I'd rather be standing on my head than playing these stories to these unfortunate people…!

MR TWIT. Enough of these interruptions!

MONKEY DAUGHTER. It's cruel, Mr Twit!

MR TWIT. Quiet!!

MONKEY SON. There are others, you know!

MRS TWIT. Don't you dare speak!

MONKEY DAD. Quiet, son!

MONKEY SON. They're out there in the darkness looking at us!

MRS TWIT. What are you talking about?! Others out where?!

MR TWIT. MUSIC!

MR TWIT *points his shotgun at the* MONKEYS.

'Pomp and Circumstance March' begins to play.

MR TWIT *encourages the* GUESTS *to do some morris dancing.*

Meanwhile MRS TWIT *is peering out into the darkness. Is there really something out there?*

Suddenly she walks quickly to the edge of the stage.

The house lights come up – the stage lights and sound are immediately cut.

In silence MRS TWIT *stands staring at us – in shock.*

Then –

MRS TWIT (*shouts*). MR TWIT!

She reaches into the darkness behind her and drags her husband into her light.

He's faced away from us.

(*Snaps.*) Turn around!

MR TWIT *turns – and he too is utterly bewildered.*

(*Whispers to him.*) What does this mean, Mr Twit?

A pause in which trepidation turns to –

MR TWIT. It means, Mrs Twit – we're going to have some fun.

The TWITS *laugh like demented schoolkids.*

Blackout.

End of Act One.

ACT TWO

The start of the second half.

To the beautiful strains of 'In the Bleak Midwinter' – snow falls.

The HANDSOME WALTZER BOY *is alone in the garden. Depressed.*

A robin lands on the branch of the tree and begins to sing.

Almost immediately this singing begins to brighten the HANDSOME WALTZER BOY*'s mood.*

A bunny rabbit appears and hops around – feeding on the grass.

Overhead and the HANDSOME WALTZER BOY *can hear something – magpies are seen – squawking a little.*

The MONKEYS *in their cage are trying to scare off the magpies from landing on the glued branches.*

The birds fly off.

The HANDSOME WALTZER BOY *sees this.*

He and the MONKEY DAUGHTER *look at one another.*

She holds up her hand to him – a sign of an apology for his story she played.

The robin singing louder now.

The HANDSOME WALTZER BOY *quickly looks back at him. The robin seems to be in real distress.*

He quickly goes to the robin – takes it gently in his hands – and tries to pick it up. It's stuck! Stuck good.

With some effort he walks backwards holding the robin – glue stretching ridiculously across the space.

The bunny rabbit is taking a real interest in this.

The HANDSOME WALTZER BOY *looks down at the rabbit.*

The sound of a shotgun being set – the HANDSOME
WALTZER BOY *slowly looking in its direction.*

*Suddenly a shotgun noise – and the rabbit is blown right off the
stage – the* HANDSOME WALTZER BOY *lets go of the robin
and it catapults in the other direction.*

'In the Bleak Midwinter' is aggressively cut.

MR TWIT (*offstage*). Got it!!

    The HANDSOME WALTZER BOY *sheepishly turns to his
friends as they approach him.*

    They're staring nervously out at us.

    The TATTOOED FORTUNE-TELLER LADY *is elected to
say something first.*

TATTOOED FORTUNE-TELLER LADY. My friends and I
have been here in this garden for – how long have we been
here?

YORKSHIRE TERRIER MAN. Months now.

TATTOOED FORTUNE-TELLER LADY. Aye, months.

HANDSOME WALTZER BOY. Seems like more.

TATTOOED FORTUNE-TELLER LADY. For a considerable
amount of time, let's say – waiting here – watching the
seasons pass and teased often by these monkeys…

YORKSHIRE TERRIER MAN. These *horrible* monkeys!

HANDSOME WALTZER BOY. They may not be as horrible as
we first thought.

TATTOOED FORTUNE-TELLER LADY. The jury's out on the
monkeys.

HANDSOME WALTZER BOY. Right.

YORKSHIRE TERRIER MAN. But it's not all been bad, lads!

HANDSOME WALTZER BOY. It's been mostly bad!

TATTOOED FORTUNE-TELLER LADY. What they did to our
friend back at Hallowe'en – the delight they got from his
miserable story…!!

YORKSHIRE TERRIER MAN. Look, it'll be Christmas Day
soon – and though we're tired and a little bit broken –

TATTOOED FORTUNE-TELLER LADY. And sick to death of
bird pie!!

YORKSHIRE TERRIER MAN. And sick of bird pie yeah – but
what better day of the year to stand in the garden and see our
fairground carried and delivered right here in front of us!
Imagine that Christmas present, pals!

The HANDSOME WALTZER BOY *is not ready to be lifted
from his depression.*

HANDSOME WALTZER BOY. Seriously – I'm cracking up.
Somethin's gotta give – I can feel it.

YORKSHIRE TERRIER MAN. Don't. Come on – stay
positive.

HANDSOME WALTZER BOY. I can't find that voice to fight
back – but I must somehow. We have to.

YORKSHIRE TERRIER MAN. The dream of holding that new
puppy is just around the corner!

The YORKSHIRE TERRIER MAN *takes the* HANDSOME
WALTZER BOY *back to the caravan.*

TATTOOED FORTUNE-TELLER LADY. Hey, I think I know
what these faces might be!

YORKSHIRE TERRIER MAN. Aye, what's that?

TATTOOED FORTUNE-TELLER LADY. Witnesses.
Witnesses to our downfall!

The TATTOOED FORTUNE-TELLER LADY *turns and
walks towards us – as her two friends return to the caravan.*

I can't go on lying like this! There's somethin' I need to talk
out to you – of course maybe the words might fail – you see
often I find it easier to say things in song – but unfortunately
I have no way of breakin' into song 'cause I've got no
musical instruments so…

*Suddenly a spotlight comes up on a piano that's suspended
overhead.*

What's this?!

A piano is lowered into the downstage.

Unbelievably – floatin' down towards me is this huge...

The piano is landing on the ground – it is a toddler's tiny grand piano (two-feet tall).

...is this piano.

She sits at the piano – looking like a giant.

This must be a sign, right? (*Slight pause.*) Right then!

She begins to play the piano – wonderfully – and starts to sing her song, 'The Club of the World's Greatest Liars'.

Now if you're paying attention –
You guessed I've got a dire secret
A secret sure to shake our bond –
A story I can't mention
A lie I told that fatal day –
It's grown all big inside a' me
It fills me with an ulcerous tension
I'm no longer a good friend
I'm more like a decidedly deceitful friend.

And standing in this crisis
With this lie that needs upending...
I am just about to become one a' the annual buyers
To the Club of the World's Greatest Liars?

Inside that horrid club – there's the –

Man who faked his own death
'Cause he needed a few bob
There's the nun who plays it saintly
When she's always on the rob
And the lass who struts in Dior
When her vest is made of string
And the bloke who pumps his body
To help his javelin fling
And there's the 'chosen ones'
Who spin to steal your votes
They'd lie in every breath
To save their sacred goats. Oh!

Is that now me? – A liar to the core
Or can I leave this Liars' Club
'Cause surely there is more –
To life.

But there's the –
Lass who's cheatin' lovers
'Cause she's fond of breakin' hearts
There's the bloke who's nickin' pennies
From 'The Fund to Save St Bart's'
And the granddad with his easel
Paints Vermeers by the load
And the chef who's fillin' meat pies
With eels and rotten toad! Ew!
And I'm the one
Who's lying to her friends
And scared of what they'll say
For what the future sends
'Cause here I stand
A liar cooked right through
Time to leave the Liars' Club
And see what I can do.

Tell the truth – no longer pretend
Stop the lie – and start a new trend
Don't fear the future – it's nearly the end
It'll be good for me ulcers – to be a good friend!

*Her song finished and she steps away from the tiny grand
piano.*

She watches it lifted back into space and calls upwards –

Thanks for that!

In darkness –

MR TWIT (*through the loudspeaker*). IT'S CHRISTMAS!

Lights up on MR *and* MRS TWIT *and the* MONKEYS.

Throughout Christmas Day – the MONKEYS *work tirelessly
as stage management.*

MRS TWIT (*brightly*). Merry merry merry merry merry
merrymerrymerrymerrymerhmerhmerhmermersh! MERRY

CHRISTMAS, dear guests! (*Out to audience*.) And isn't it joyful to be joined by so many unusual faces, Mr Twit?!

MR TWIT. It is joyful and yet perplexing to be faced by this new reality, Mrs Twit.

MR TWIT *quickly grabs his shotgun.*

MRS TWIT. If I didn't have this terrible aversion to touching humans I would poke one of them to see if they were real.

MR TWIT. Engaging them in actual communication – is an idea best avoided.

MRS TWIT. And why's that, you old fruit?!

MR TWIT. Their numbers are too large and communication would risk criticism or worse still – friendship.

MRS TWIT. Best to keep them at arm's length and seduce them with our charms, Mr Twit?

MR TWIT. Our charms and our affability – and when we are wanting in both of those properties we can always win their favour with delicious sweets!

MRS TWIT. Monkey Daughter!!

MONKEY DAUGHTER *chucks sweets* (*three of them, one at a time*) *into the audience.*

MR TWIT. Humans love sweets.

MRS TWIT. They absolutely adore them.

MR TWIT. And how on earth did you make these sugary delights, Mrs Twit?

MRS TWIT. Oh you can pulverise, roll into balls and deep-fry anything you like.

YORKSHIRE TERRIER MAN. We're still here you know!

The TWITS *turn around fast* –

MR TWIT. Well how awfully nice to see you again – isn't it nice, Mrs Twit?!

MRS TWIT. It's positively wonderful to see them again, Mr Twit.

MR TWIT. After all these days – how lovely!

HANDSOME WALTZER BOY. We want to go home!

MR TWIT. But aren't you 'home' – isn't that what you call that thing?!

HANDSOME WALTZER BOY. We've done enough waiting – we want to leave, right now! Right this second!

MR TWIT. And back to living beneath a flyover – in *Leeds*??!! My God, man – where's your ambition?! Music!

A version of 'O Little Town of Bethlehem' as remixed by Slade is heard.

They are all made to sing.

ALL (*singing*). O little town of Bethlehem
How still we see thee lie!
Above your deep and dreamless sleep
The silent stars go by
Yet in thy dark streets shineth

MRS TWIT *wants it louder.*

The everlasting light
The hopes and fears of all the years
Are met in thee tonight –

MR TWIT. Lyrics!

MONKEY DAD *unravels a banner with the lyrics for the audience to sing along badly scrawled on it.*

ALL (*singing*). O morning stars together
Proclaim the holy birth –   '

During this the MONKEY DAUGHTER *has got closer to the* HANDSOME WALTZER BOY. *He looks at her.*

MONKEY DAUGHTER. We're good monkeys – I promise ya.

HANDSOME WALTZER BOY. I know you are.

ALL (*singing*). And praises sing – (*Etc.*)

During all this MRS TWIT *leaves the stage.*

The song thankfully ends with an explosion of sparkle activated by MONKEY MAM.

MR TWIT (*to someone in the front row*). You like a Christmas carol, do you? Gives you a warm fuzzy feeling in your belly, does it? You like to hear children raucously sing about peace and harmony – and baby Jesus?

Then from the depths of his soul –

I used to be a child. Miserable adventure. (*Calls.*) Monkeys!!

MONKEY DAD *and* SON *play a fanfare on kazoos – while* MONKEY DAUGHTER *carries* MRS TWIT *onto the stage on a wooden hand-trolley* (*Hannibal Lector-style*).

She is costumed as Queen Elizabeth II.

MRS TWIT. Lightslightlightslightsslightstestess – hytestesteslightstestesslightstestesslightstestess…

A light comes down on MRS TWIT *as she delivers her Christmas message –*

To look back is not always to be nostalgic – people of Great Britain – and its colonies. I shall never forget the Christmases of my youth. Back then I was a child. And like so many children I was very often annoying. I demanded too much from my parents. And not just bread and drinking water but other luxuries too. This insatiable greed for all things turned me into a spoilt-little-piggy around Christmas time. They say that children are the most precious things in life. But that's just complete rubbish. Children very often make life 'challenging' and 'miserable'. A child's inquisitive nature can turn daily existence into a relentless annoyance. A shy child, who hides away and reads quietly in their bedroom – is nothing more than a pretentious bed-wetter. And is there anything more atrocious in the world than a confident, expressive, flamboyant child? (*Thinks, retches and pukes a little into a handkerchief.*) I don't think there is. (*With increasing anger.*) An attention-grabbing spirited child – filling a room with their childish wonder – can often induce illness! I myself am known to expel large amounts of puke – as soon as a child begins to exPRESS ANYTHING MORE THAN A BREATH…!

Suddenly MRS TWIT *is struck in the face with a frying pan.*

Lights up full and MR TWIT *holds a vibrating frying pan, his wife holding her face.*

MR TWIT. That's enough of that! Anyone else want to make a speech?

MR TWIT *looks out at us.*

Anyone? Light, Monkey Daughter, light!!

MONKEY DAUGHTER *shines a torch into the audience.*

(*To audience.*) No need to be shy – we're all friends here. Just a tiny recital, maybe? Or a small whimsical anecdote? Anyone? (*Slight pause.*) Anything at all?

He quickly turns around to the TATTOOED FORTUNE-TELLER LADY.

How about you – Tattooed Fortune-Teller Lady? Anything of your sad past that you'd like to share?

She tries to gather some courage…

I didn't think so! Bring in the festive dinner!

MONKEY DAD *and* SON *wheel in a life-sized roasted deer – antlers still attached.*

(*To audience.*) Ohh we all love Christmas dinner, don't we!

Dumbfounded and the GUESTS *just stare at the roasted deer.*

Then –

HANDSOME WALTZER BOY. Is that who I think it is?

MR TWIT. In the dark night sky – he was betrayed by the one thing that made him so beloved by children.

Suddenly the deer's red nose lights up.

YORKSHIRE TERRIER MAN. Oh bloomin' 'eck!

MR TWIT. I had to reload twice – the damn buck.

MRS TWIT. He did stuff quite easily, mind you. Plenty of elbow room in good ol' Rudolph!

MRS TWIT *snaps off a bit of antler and eats it like crackling.*

Just like chicken!

HANDSOME WALTZER BOY (*snaps*). ENOUGH OF THIS! ENOUGH!! It is one thing keepin' us here with the dwindling hope of getting back our fairground and feedin' us revolting bird pie – but to attack Christmas?! A time of year when we're all reminded of the importance of love and family!

YORKSHIRE TERRIER MAN. You know nothin' about fellowship, about friends and community, do you?!

HANDSOME WALTZER BOY. Nothing!

MONKEY DAD. Look how you treat my family!

HANDSOME WALTZER BOY. Exactly! Look how you treat these superbly talented family of monkey-actors!!

MRS TWIT. They're working, aren't they?!

MONKEY DAD. You hate us 'cause we love each other!

MONKEY MAM. You hate the idea of love!

YORKSHIRE TERRIER MAN. It's like you see no strength in love!

HANDSOME WALTZER BOY. Christmas tells us that we are human beings and monkeys – that together – as family and friends – as a community – we can overcome whatever hardships life fires at us…

MR TWIT *shoots his potato gun into the* HANDSOME WALTZER BOY*'s eye.*

OWWW!!

The MONKEY DAUGHTER *whispers in the* HANDSOME WALTZER BOY*'s ear –*

MONKEY DAUGHTER. You really think we're superbly talented?

HANDSOME WALTZER BOY. Yeah.

MONKEY DAUGHTER. What lovely teeth you have.

HANDSOME WALTZER BOY. Thanks.

She suddenly grabs his face and kisses him vigorously. He makes a little yelping noise.

She jolts back – holding one of his front teeth in her mouth.

You sucked out my tooth!

MONKEY DAUGHTER (*placing it in her purse*). I'll give it back to ya once I finish with it.

MR TWIT *stands close to the* TATTOOED FORTUNE-TELLER LADY –

MR TWIT (*whispers*). We will not have a revolt on our hands! Say something to them! You've been lying all these years – no need to stop lying now!

The phone rings.

Everyone looks towards it.

(*To the* TATTOOED FORTUNE-TELLER LADY.) Go on – answer it.

The TATTOOED FORTUNE-TELLER LADY *slowly walks towards the telephone and answers it.*

TATTOOED FORTUNE-TELLER LADY. Hello. (*Pause.*) Oh yeah? Great. Thanks.

She places down the phone.

YORKSHIRE TERRIER MAN. Was there really a man at the other end of that phone?

TATTOOED FORTUNE-TELLER LADY. Yeah.

HANDSOME WALTZER BOY. So what did he say?

She lies convincingly –

TATTOOED FORTUNE-TELLER LADY. That he's really very close.

YORKSHIRE TERRIER MAN. He really said that?

She almost breaks.

MR TWIT. And did he say something nice about the fairground he's delivering? (*Slight pause.*) Well?

TATTOOED FORTUNE-TELLER LADY. He said it looks really great.

YORKSHIRE TERRIER MAN (*elated*). Oh my God!

MR TWIT. And what else did he say?

A slight pause.

TATTOOED FORTUNE-TELLER LADY. That it's just the same as we remember it.

HANDSOME WALTZER BOY (*overcome*). Oh that is the greatest news, isn't it, love?

TATTOOED FORTUNE-TELLER LADY. It is, yeah.

MR TWIT. How lovely!!

MRS TWIT. Now let's eat before Rudolph gets cold!!

The loud syncopated rhythm returns.

The GUESTS *are escorted back into the caravan by* MR TWIT.

Before she goes in – he grabs the TATTOOED FORTUNE-TELLER LADY *by the arm – and kisses her forcibly on the cheek.*

MRS TWIT *sits astride Rudolph and rips meat off his neck and eats it.*

MR TWIT *orders the* MONKEYS *back inside their cage.*

MR TWIT. On your heads – on your heads!

He turns and pushes the roasted reindeer and his wife off into the wings.

The music ends.

A spring morning and slowly the caravan door opens.

The TATTOOED FORTUNE-TELLER LADY *appears outside – she's carrying a little suitcase.*

Her small bit of courage, vanished now – and it's time for her to leave.

The MONKEYS *in their cage are seen in the downstage. They are singing 'Calon Lân' –*

MONKEYS. Nid wy'n gofyn bywyd moethus,
　　Aur y byd na'i berlau mân:
　　Gofyn wyf am galon hapus,
　　Calon onest, calon lân.

　　Calon lân yn llawn daioni,
　　Tecach yw na'r lili dlos:
　　Dim ond calon lân all ganu –
　　Canu'r dydd a chanu'r nos.

　　Pe dymunwn olud bydol,
　　Hedyn buan ganddo sydd;
　　Golud calon lân, rinweddol,
　　Yn dwyn bythol elw fydd.

　　Hwyr a bore fy nymuniad
　　Gwyd i'r nef ar edyn cân
　　Ar i Dduw, er mwyn fy Ngheidwad,
　　Roddi i mi galon lân.

MONKEY DAUGHTER. Will you say it again, Mam?

MONKEY SON. One more time, come on.

MONKEY MAM. Really?

MONKEY DAD. Please, pet.

　　As MONKEY MAM *talks, the* TATTOOED FORTUNE-
　　TELLER LADY *stands – unseen – listening to her.*

MONKEY MAM. It will be a spring day as it is now – and the
　　field where our tree is – will be covered with yellow
　　daffodils – and the tree where our new house will be – will
　　have branches filled with buds ready to pop inta life. And
　　through the window of our little house you'll see us all sat
　　around our table – and we're drinking tea and eating cakes –
　　and we're singing a song to welcome in the day. (*Slight
　　pause*.) Never fully beaten. There'll always be a new
　　morning.

HANDSOME WALTZER BOY. You're up and about early.

　　The TATTOOED FORTUNE-TELLER LADY *turns around
　　and sees the* YORKSHIRE TERRIER MAN *and*
　　HANDSOME WALTZER BOY *stepping out of the caravan,
　　walking towards her.*

YORKSHIRE TERRIER MAN. What ya doin' – excited over our fairground's imminent arrival?

HANDSOME WALTZER BOY. Has there been another phone call from that delivery man?

TATTOOED FORTUNE-TELLER LADY. No not really.

She badly hides her suitcase.

YORKSHIRE TERRIER MAN. I imagine there's no point phoning now – he's probably within shouting distance!

HANDSOME WALTZER BOY. Yeah right.

A pause. Then –

TATTOOED FORTUNE-TELLER LADY. Look, why not take a seat, friends – there's something I need to tell ya.

HANDSOME WALTZER BOY. Tell us what?

YORKSHIRE TERRIER MAN. What ya mean…?

TATTOOED FORTUNE-TELLER LADY. I'm going to tell you my story – and though it will upset you some – at its finish – you'll know the truth about me and the twenty-fourth of May in Great Missenden. Then, friends – I'm prayin' for forgiveness and a new start with ya. A new morning.

The two men are very worried now.

YORKSHIRE TERRIER MAN. All right then, love. We're ready. (*Slight pause.*) Let's have it then.

HANDSOME WALTZER BOY. Let us hear – your final day.

A slight pause.

TATTOOED FORTUNE-TELLER LADY. I woke in my little caravan…

Suddenly the MONKEYS *appear and unfurl a banner reading – 'FORTUNE-TELLER. TIME AT HER FINGERTIPS! 5 tokens'.*

HANDSOME WALTZER BOY. Who let the monkeys out?

TATTOOED FORTUNE-TELLER LADY. Don't know. Seems like they're trying to help.

She restarts her story.

I woke…

*Suddenly the terrifying sound of a carousel begins playing –
and over the loudspeakers –*

MR TWIT. She woke in her little caravan to the sounds of the
fairground outside –

The MONKEYS *open the caravan door and* MR *and* MRS
TWIT *are waiting inside.*

– the air charged with anticipation – the good people of
Great Missenden filling their pockets with money to spend.

MRS TWIT. She sat as she did every morning with time at her
fingertips – and what tantalising glimpses into the future
would she and her crystal ball give to the good people of
Great Missenden?

Seated between them and the TATTOOED FORTUNE-
TELLER LADY *is handed a large potato –*

TATTOOED FORTUNE-TELLER LADY. Oh what magical
history I hold in my hands! For legend has it – that this
crystal ball was formed from the tears of 'The Goddesses of
Fate'. From Ancient Greece it came and rolled about Europe
giving truths to people who were willin' to part with a fiver
for a chance of tricking time.

MR TWIT. And while she sat there boasting of her great power
– two titans were sitting in their Chrysler Avenger.

MRS TWIT. We sat there sketching.

MR TWIT. Scheming. Mixing.

MRS TWIT. Designing the Downfall of the Tattooed Fortune-
Teller Lady by smashing that ridiculous crystal ball –

MR TWIT. – and planning the theft of her beloved fairground.

MRS TWIT. Let us begin, Mr Twit!

MR TWIT. Yes, Mrs Twit!

MRS TWIT. Beg your pardon – but might you look into your
crystal ball and offer us some encouragement and comfort?

TATTOOED FORTUNE-TELLER LADY. Aye, of course.

MRS TWIT. Having you and your crystal ball offering us a little insight into our futures would be very educational – wouldn't it, Mr Twit?

MR TWIT (*aside to* MRS TWIT). We're here to destroy it, you old bag!

Looking into the potato –

TATTOOED FORTUNE-TELLER LADY (*suddenly*). Oh my word!!

MRS TWIT. And what is it you see?! Probably a future of glory and success, Mr Twit!

TATTOOED FORTUNE-TELLER LADY. Neither 'glory' or 'success' could be mentioned alongside these terrible visions I see right in front of me!

MRS TWIT. What?!

TATTOOED FORTUNE-TELLER LADY. For here – Mr and Mrs Twit – I see horrible torturous acts perpetrated by yourselves on one another!

MR TWIT. Stop that!!

TATTOOED FORTUNE-TELLER LADY. – and locked inside a windowless house you'll be – your union bound together by hate – and you two reduced to squabbling animals – and brought down finally by the Terrible Shrinks!

MR TWIT. Enough – ENOUGH!

MR TWIT *suddenly smashes the potato with a hammer.*

And now you see nothing!

MRS TWIT. Go, Mr Twit – do it!

MR TWIT. All your years looking into a future that should never have been looked at and you have angered time – and time is stuck outside this caravan door – events are to be repeated again and again. Do you see visions, Mrs Twit?

MRS TWIT (*with eyes shut*). The clouds are lifting and the events of this afternoon I can see clearly!

MR TWIT. And what is it you see outside?

MRS TWIT. I see a violent terrier and a large crowd watching that doggie tearing at a Yorkshireman who's reaching for his gun. I see a Waltzer Boy, his words stuck in his throat and faced by a pretty girl who's mocking this terrified stammering boy.

MR TWIT. With time stuck – are we to believe that these two people are to be imprisoned in this cruel day?

MRS TWIT. A terrible day that will play out over and over.

TATTOOED FORTUNE-TELLER LADY. Why should I believe that any of this rubbish is true!?

MR TWIT. Journey around your fairground – and see for yourself!

He shoves the TATTOOED FORTUNE-TELLER LADY *in the back – she stumbles into the fairground as the sounds escalate around her –*

TATTOOED FORTUNE-TELLER LADY (*to the* YORKSHIRE TERRIER MAN). And outside I'm walkin' through the fairground with the crowd already pulled towards you and Baxter – and pushin' against one another – and jaws droppin'– as Baxter – possessed by some poisonous evil – tears at his devoted master – and you reaching for your gun and…

Sound of a gun being fired twice – the TWITS *are seen taping the sounds on an old recorder.*

I turn away from that terrifying noise – the Twits' prophecy pushin' like a knife inta my throat. (*To the* HANDSOME WALTZER BOY.) I can see the prettiest girl in Great Missenden – her horrible laughter fired towards you – your words jammed in your throat – your heart ripped out by that awful humiliation! I turn and run! RUN!

The sounds of mocking laughter – and again the TWITS *are seen taping this.*

And if this day is to repeat itself – then my two best friends in the whole world will be tortured by these cruel scenes for eternity! To the caravan I return fast – the noises drillin' me back into the inside!

She enters the bubble caravan.

MRS TWIT. And is it true – are your friends to be stuck in this terrible day for ever?

MR TWIT. If you want to undo the badness you've done in your life –

MR TWIT *holds out a contract and a pen –*

Sign the fairground over to me.

A slight pause.

TATTOOED FORTUNE-TELLER LADY. I won't do that!

MR TWIT. Then take a listen outside! Mrs Twit!

MRS TWIT *opens up the caravan door – hits her tape recorder – the looping sound of gunshot and pretty girls laughing is heard.*

MR TWIT *shoves the* TATTOOED FORTUNE-TELLER LADY*'s head out the window.*

Sign it! Sign it!

TATTOOED FORTUNE-TELLER LADY. Make it stop, please! I'll do anything you ask!

MR TWIT. It's your abuse of time that's imprisoned your friends outside! Give us the fairground and set them free!!

MR *and* MRS TWIT. Sign it! Sign it! SIGN IT!

Finally snapping – and she grabs the contract from MR TWIT *and signs it.*

TATTOOED FORTUNE-TELLER LADY. I sign it to free you of this eternal curse –

She leaves the caravan and turns back to see –

MR TWIT. A wonderful trick, Mrs Twit.

They laugh into the tape recorder.

TATTOOED FORTUNE-TELLER LADY. But I was tricked! In signin' that contract I sign away our beloved fairground to those terrible Twits – and consign our lives to failure!

The TWITS *remain in the caravan – the sounds and music and the* TATTOOED FORTUNE-TELLER LADY *– collapse in on themselves – the story finished as she faces her two friends.*

Silence and stillness.

The YORKSHIRE TERRIER MAN *and the* HANDSOME WALTZER BOY *stand, barely containing their anger –*

HANDSOME WALTZER BOY. Is this what happened? Is this true?

TATTOOED FORTUNE-TELLER LADY. Yeah.

YORKSHIRE TERRIER MAN. All these years you've been tellin' us that the Twits stole the fairground from us… but ya just gave it to them?

TATTOOED FORTUNE-TELLER LADY. I did it to save you two – they tricked me into doin' it – you just saw that! They tricked the three of us! They planned it all to make me sign!

HANDSOME WALTZER BOY. Whether you were tricked or not – you could have told us the truth back then!

TATTOOED FORTUNE-TELLER LADY. Yeah and for that I'm sorry – really I am!

YORKSHIRE TERRIER MAN. Had we got the fairground back that first day we came here – you'd never have told us…

TATTOOED FORTUNE-TELLER LADY. I might 'ave…

YORKSHIRE TERRIER MAN. You came here wantin' to bury that lie!

HANDSOME WALTZER BOY (*grabbing her suitcase*). And what about you sneakin' off just now – takin' that lie with ya, probably!

TATTOOED FORTUNE-TELLER LADY. But I stayed to tell yas the truth, didn't I?!

During the below – MR *and* MRS TWIT *are putting saucepans into the* GUESTS' *hands.*

YORKSHIRE TERRIER MAN. But only now you're tellin' us the truth! Why not back then on that mornin' when we woke up and we found the fairground gone?! Why not tell us the truth then?!

TATTOOED FORTUNE-TELLER LADY. I had to tell you they stole it – I was ashamed to say I gave it to them! I was humiliated – confused…

YORKSHIRE TERRIER MAN. We're supposed to be friends, aren't we?!

TATTOOED FORTUNE-TELLER LADY. Don't be daft – of course we're friends!

YORKSHIRE TERRIER MAN. But friends tell the truth to one another! Without truth between us – there's nothing!

TATTOOED FORTUNE-TELLER LADY. Stop it…

HANDSOME WALTZER BOY. You lied on Christmas Day about the fairground comin' back, didn't ya?! There was no man on the other end of that telephone…

TATTOOED FORTUNE-TELLER LADY. I were buying time, that's all!

YORKSHIRE TERRIER MAN. It's cruel what you've done to us! What we've suffered in this garden! You're a liar!!

YORKSHIRE TERRIER MAN *and* HANDSOME WALTZER BOY. LIAR LIAR!!

TATTOOED FORTUNE-TELLER LADY. Stop it! STOP!!

They go to strike each other with the saucepans.

This sad image is held for a moment.

MR TWIT. Well this is all very depressing, isn't it, Mrs Twit?

MRS TWIT. Oh please stop teasing them and give them back their beloved fairground – surely now's the right time. Please, Mr Twit.

MR TWIT. But what lesson have they all learnt, Mrs Twit?

MRS TWIT. What lesson? That there is no 'friendship' – there is no 'family' – there is no 'unity'. They're stuck together by their nothingness.

MR TWIT. An excellent summary, Mrs Twit! (*Announcing*.) Now, dear guests – the fairground – returneth!

From somewhere, MRS TWIT *pulls a lever – and beneath the ground – smashed and hidden and buried in the garden – the fairground lights barely illuminate.*

Right under your noses all this time.

MRS TWIT. It's been a wonderful trick, hasn't it, Mr Twit?

MR TWIT. Quite possibly our best ever trick, Mrs Twit. Now – you broken despicable people –

MRS TWIT. – stew inside that pokey caravan of yours –

MR TWIT. – hate one another –

MRS TWIT. – eat your bird pie –

MR TWIT. – and meditate on your worthlessness!

That loud syncopated rhythm returns as the GUESTS *are driven back into the caravan – the door jammed shut by* MRS TWIT*'s walking stick.*

The MONKEYS *are forced back into their cage.*

With MR *and* MRS TWIT *gone – the music stops.*

Time passes through the night – MONKEY DAUGHTER *is filing the* HANDSOME WALTZER BOY*'s tooth and working on her constructed key – as her family sleep around her.*

She raises the new key aloft – it's finished.

MONKEY DAUGHTER (*loud whisper*). It's done! I've only gone and blinkin' done it again!

She reaches her hand out of the cage, places the key in the lock and opens the cage door –

MONKEYS. *Un, dau, tri.*

They step outside and into their freedom.

The MONKEYS *are about to escape the garden wall – when* MONKEY DAD *looks towards the bubble caravan.*

He turns and faces his family. They all know what to do.

MONKEY DAD. Right now we could be over the garden wall – we could be running through Buckinghamshire – through fields and forests – acquainting ourselves with the English wildlife, with those weird native animals they call…?

MONKEY SON. Hedgehogs.

MONKEY DAD. Right!

MONKEY DAUGHTER. We could be setting up a monkey house for ourselves with the various and most up-to-date monkey accessories – but we're not going to do any of that, are we, Dad?

MONKEY SON. Not just yet we're not!

MONKEY MAM. It would feel like freedom in that forest – but it wouldn't be. In the minds of the Twits – we'd always be these terrified upside-down monkeys.

MONKEY DAD. And they'd always be the broken owners of a broken fairground.

The MONKEYS *hop up on top of the caravan and hammer the roof.*

MONKEY SON. The Twits must be beaten!

YORKSHIRE TERRIER MAN. We can't beat them.

MONKEY DAD. Together we can!

TATTOOED FORTUNE-TELLER LADY. They're cleverer than all of us – they've proved that.

MONKEY DAUGHTER. They're not clever – they're Twits!

HANDSOME WALTZER BOY. We're broken people!

MONKEY MAM. Broken but not dead in the ground, surely?!

MONKEY DAUGHTER. You have a heartbeat, don't you?!

TATTOOED FORTUNE-TELLER LADY. Well barely!

MONKEY MAM. And you have each other!

YORKSHIRE TERRIER MAN. We don't even have that any more!

TATTOOED FORTUNE-TELLER LADY. Maybe we deserve to be where we are! They knocked us down and split us up and kept us here – so maybe stuck here arguin' self-worth with a family of monkeys is as good as it gets for people like us.

MONKEY DAUGHTER. Oh that's harsh.

MONKEY DAD. It was hope that brought you here and maybe pathetic hope that held you here – but it is hope that can still set you free!

MONKEY DAUGHTER *puts down a tin of Hugtight Glue in front of the* HANDSOME WALTZER BOY.

HANDSOME WALTZER BOY. Where are the Twits?

MONKEY DAUGHTER. It's springtime and the lambing season.

MONKEY SON. They'll be out hunting lambs.

MONKEY MAM. They'll be back soon!

HANDSOME WALTZER BOY. Monkey Dad and his family are right, friends! Right now we're divided and sad, yeah?… But we are still people, aren't we? People and talkin' monkeys… but we are all of us individual creatures – who still have a life. No one person is greater than the other – and those who see themselves as superior – as bein' entitled to a better way of life – through heritage or money – those who trick and keep the quiet ones down – they must be reminded that cruelness and bullyin' will never win out! It's not their world to run as they wish – to make rules, shove us inta boxes – pull us out like puppets and fob us off with terrible acting jobs and disgustin' bird pie – when we are a community, friends! Staying together we are larger and smarter and more powerful than they can ever wish to be! Do not allow your fear to chain you any longer – we must rise up and build a new world where we are all equal – where hope can set us free – where we can all dream big dreams!

The MONKEY DAUGHTER *is up close and now whispers in his ear –*

MONKEY DAUGHTER. You are so attractive to me right now.

Again she kisses him for some moments.

The kiss breaks and he sees that his front tooth has returned.

HANDSOME WALTZER BOY. My tooth's back.

MONKEY DAUGHTER. A monkey will always keep her promise.

The GUESTS *and the other* MONKEYS *turn and look at us.*

MONKEY DAD. We owe it to all those witnesses out there. What we do today – is our legacy.

A slight pause.

YORKSHIRE TERRIER MAN (*to the* TATTOOED FORTUNE-TELLER LADY). What's the one thing the Twits would hate more than anythin' else, comrade?

TATTOOED FORTUNE-TELLER LADY. To be shown to the whole world – for the Twits that they are.

The syncopated rhythm returns.

The TWITS *are seen shooting lambs. The two lambs they've already shot are draped over their shoulders.*

During the below – without been seen by the TWITS *– the* MONKEYS *have brushed glue onto the* TWITS' *heads.*

The rhythm lowers in volume as they talk –

MRS TWIT. Well that was enjoyable, wasn't it, Mr Twit?

MR TWIT. Nothing like an afternoon hunting lamb to build up an appetite for more destruction.

MRS TWIT. The bleating of lambs and gunfire – there is no sweeter sound to welcome spring. But tell me, you old sack of muck – do you ever tire of torturing the weak?

MR TWIT. Tire of torturing the weak – what on earth are you jabbering on about!? Having absolutely no regard for life and hating every living creature on this miserable planet of ours – is something of which I will never tire.

You are either 'us' or 'them' – and let me remind you, you old fish – you don't want to be weak and you don't want to be kind – you want to be strong, powerful and always right and whERE'S-THE-FURNITURE!?

MRS TWIT *screams.*

Shut it…!

But MRS TWIT *continues screaming.*

He goes to jam her mouth with his shotgun – but even he wouldn't do that.

He rips a hoof off the lamb he's just shot and shoves it in her gob.

Silence.

MR TWIT *slowly looks out to the audience.*

(*Smiling.*) Well, my new friends – is this your little joke? (*Fake-laughs. Fails. Stops.*) How very very very very very – funny.

Suddenly something is appearing (rumbling) overhead.

All their furniture is on the ceiling.

MR *and* MRS TWIT *look up.*

MRS TWIT. That's the floor! That's the floor up there!

MR TWIT. I can see it's the floor!

MRS TWIT. This is the ceiling! We're standing on the ceiling, Mr Twit!

MR TWIT. We're upside down! We're standing on the ceiling looking at the floor! I don't like this one bit! What's happening here?! What's happening…!?

MRS TWIT. We're upside down and all the blood's going to my head! If we don't do something quickly, I shall die, I know I will!

MR TWIT. I know what we'll do! We'll stand on our heads – and that way we'll be the right way up!

They both stand on their heads.

Absolutely perfect.

MONKEY DAD. Hello there, Mr Twit.

MONKEY DAD (*holding the tin of Hugtight Glue*) *stands with his family on one side of the stage –*

MR TWIT. You're upside down – you stupid chimp!! Just the way I like you!

HANDSOME WALTZER BOY. Or is it you who's the stupid one?

The TATTOOED FORTUNE-TELLER LADY, HANDSOME WALTZER BOY *and* YORKSHIRE TERRIER MAN *stand on the other side of the stage.*

MR TWIT. What are you doing out of your cages!? Back in your caravan, you plebs!

MRS TWIT. My head's stuck! My head's stuck!

MR TWIT. What?!

MRS TWIT. They've stuck our heads! I can smell glue, Mr Twit!

MR TWIT. Unstick our heads this very moment!

MRS TWIT. Why aren't you inside that box of yours – hating one another!?

YORKSHIRE TERRIER MAN. Because we have somethin' you've never had.

MR TWIT. And what's that – a pathetic, miserable life?!

MRS TWIT. Oooouuuuusssshhkkkkkkkeeeeee...

MR TWIT. Unstick our heads, I said!!

HANDSOME WALTZER BOY. We have friendship –

YORKSHIRE TERRIER MAN. – we have togetherness – you horrible little twits.

MR TWIT. There's nothing *little* about us!

MRS TWIT. Shheeekkkaaaaaaaa...

MR TWIT. We're big and strong and incredibly powerful!

MRS TWIT. Shomethins aa happeninnn, Ma Twit!

MR TWIT. Will you be quiet – you silly old cow!

A light comes down on the TWITS *as they wriggle and squirm and choggle – but with each movement they are disappearing into their bodies.*

MRS TWIT. Da Shrinks – da Drweaded Shrinks!!

MR TWIT. NO NO DA SHRINKKKKKSSSSSSS…

Despite their heads disappearing into their bodies – their desperate cries can still be heard.

But eventually – their grizzly passing – ends.

The TWITS *are no more.*

Only two small nasty brown stains remain.

The light widens and the MONKEYS *and the* GUESTS *look across at each other.*

Then –

MONKEY SON. What is this feeling I'm feeling in my belly, Dad?

MONKEY DAD. Explain it to me.

MONKEY SON. It's like a fluttering inside but also a ballooning and it's filling me up without giving me too much discomfort.

MONKEY DAD. It sounds like wind, son.

MONKEY MAM. It's happiness.

MONKEY DAD. Or happiness. Most definitely happiness. It's over.

MONKEY MAM. Oh it feels so good, doesn't it, love?

MONKEY DAD. It does.

HANDSOME WALTZER BOY. It feels like what you imagine love should be like.

MONKEY DAUGHTER. Have you noticed that you don't stammer around me like you might do with other pretty girls?

HANDSOME WALTZER BOY. I think it's because you're a monkey.

MONKEY DAUGHTER. Or maybe – you just met the right girl – who happens to be a monkey.

HANDSOME WALTZER BOY (*smiles*). Yeah maybe.

They hold hands.

YORKSHIRE TERRIER MAN. On this spring morning – the world has opened right up to us, friends. Beyond that wall is Buckinghamshire – and England too – and the possibility of a new puppy barking for me. And who knows – but maybe this very day we will dig up the remains of our beloved fairground – we will mend and paint all these broken parts and travel once again through this beautiful countryside of ours. Never again will we say these two words – 'The Twits' – we will travel and lose ourselves in the joy and love and community of our fellow countrymen and women.

A slight pause.

HANDSOME WALTZER BOY (*to the* TATTOOED FORTUNE-TELLER LADY). Are you all right, love.

She's been quiet all this time.

TATTOOED FORTUNE-TELLER LADY. Yeah. Yeah of course. (*Slight pause.*) I just wish I could put into words how big a feeling I'm feeling right now. But 'love', 'happy', 'proud' – seem like terribly flat words, don't they?

MONKEY SON. They do sound rubbish.

TATTOOED FORTUNE-TELLER LADY. In times like this – I find only song can really express how we all feel right now.

MONKEY SON. Well we've got something, hey, Mam?

MONKEY MAM. Right, son. Go on then.

MONKEY SON *plays 'Morning Has Broken' on his Casio.*

MONKEY SON *sings –*

MONKEY SON. Morning has broken, like the first morning Blackbird has spoken, like the first bird –

MONKEY MAM *and* SON. Praise for the singing, praise for
    the morning
    Praise for the springing fresh from the world –

MONKEYS. Sweet the rain's new fall, sunlit in Missenden
    Like the first dewfall, on the first grass –

A table has come out and MONKEY MAM *places a
tablecloth on it. Cake and tea and cups appear from
somewhere.*

ALL. Praise for the sweetness of the wet garden
    Sprung in completeness where our feet pass
    Ours is the sunlight, ours is this morning
    Born of the one light, England saw play
    Praise with elation, praise every morning
    Our recreation of this new day.

Lights slowly fade on this happy scene –

The End.

A Nick Hern Book

Roald Dahl's The Twits (play) first published in Great Britain in 2015 as a paperback original by Nick Hern Books Limited, The Glasshouse, 49a Goldhawk Road, London W12 8QP, in association with the Royal Court Theatre

The Twits (novel) copyright © 1980 Roald Dahl Nominee Ltd
Roald Dahl's The Twits (play) copyright © 2015 Enda Walsh

Enda Walsh has asserted his moral right to be identified as the author of this work

Image credit: Lovers

Designed and typeset by Nick Hern Books, London
Printed in Great Britain by CPI Group (UK) Ltd

A CIP catalogue record for this book is available from the British Library

ISBN 978 1 84842 474 6